Soul Sessions:

Volume 1 - Healing

for the Soul

Rhonda Ferguson- Lewis

Soul Sessions: Volume 1 – Healing for the Soul

Copyright @ 2019 Rhonda Ferguson-Lewis

Edited by Theresa Tippins & Stephanie Pop

Cover Design by Andrea A. Jordan

For booking information, please visit author's website:
www.thewinningimage.net

Foreword *(Alphabetical Order)*

Like Jacob; you may be wrestling with your past mistakes, choices, decisions or what, the Uncommon Mentor Rhonda Ferguson-Lewis calls SOUL TIES. Jacob wrestled and wouldn't let go until he was (blessed) set-free. *"Soul Sessions: Volume 1 – Healing for the Soul"* is a personal revival and with application of its contents, like Jacob you can be set-free. Rhonda Ferguson-Lewis writes from a real, relevant and relational standpoint. I encourage anyone wrestling with Soul-Ties with a desire to be set-free to read *"Soul Sessions: Volume 1 – Healing for the Soul."*

Pastor Larry Baker

Victory Church - Margate, Florida

In this Book, *"Soul Sessions: Volume 1 – Healing for the Soul,"* Rhonda Ferguson-Lewis has poured out her heart and soul in Ten Amazing Sessions. In the Bible, it doesn't use the word "soul-tie," but it speaks of them when it talks about souls being knit together, becoming one flesh. Pastor Lewis breaks down the real meaning and understanding of soul ties. In the very first session she gives a prophetic warning to "Heal Soul Wounds before they Become Soul Ties." I've been in the Pastorate for the past thirty-five years, and I have yet to read a book that has help me understand the S.E.E. (*Significant Emotional Events*) of my life as does this book. I have had the pleasure of personally knowing this author for the past almost twenty years, and she has proven to be one of the most spiritual yet practical people that I've ever known. There is a level of transparency in her life that shows up in this book. Session #5 on the Spirit of Unforgiveness will have you rebuking any and all roots of bitterness that can grow up in a person because of Unbelief. I'm very honored to have been asked to share a few words as you present this book. I am very proud of you! The Best Is Still Yet To Come!!

Reverend Dr. Alphonso Jackson, Sr.

Second Baptist Church – Richmond Heights, Florida

Pastor Rhonda Ferguson-Lewis has been a part of my life for over 16 years. The content and context of this masterpiece entitled *"Soul Sessions: Volume 1 – Healing for the Soul"* is the direct reflection and audible echo of a life that has experienced the words on every page. As I read through each session, I was captivated by the one who sets the captives free and couldn't help but realize the principle of only taking a person through and to a place that you have encountered yourself. Pastor Rhonda Ferguson-Lewis has paved the way for every person trapped by *Significant Emotional Events* to be set free once and for all through each session in this book. As you read through this book and allow the prophetic writings to place you on the examination table, know that you are not alone and that every sentence, every punctuation, and every accentuation is a derivative of a life that has passed through that very same place. Allow *"Soul Sessions: Volume 1 – Healing for the Soul"* to do the deep work in you that it was destined and created to do. Blessings on you and your journey.

Pastor D'wayne Louard

Co-Laborer at Hope International Church - Groveland, Florida

What would it profit a person to gain the treasures of this world and lose their soul? Things such as character, integrity and relationship have always been at the forefront of this author's concerns as it pertains to the growth and development of Christian believers. For years, Rhonda Ferguson-Lewis has been traveling the United States and abroad teaching, preaching, proclaiming, declaring and decreeing to let people know the importance of positive Christian living. Who and what we allow ourselves to connect with makes the difference and outcome of our lives. After working with Rhonda for several years as high school educators our classrooms were right across the hall from one another. This made it virtually impossible for us not to connect, correspond and collaborate both on a natural and spiritual level. Rhonda Ferguson-Lewis is genuine, impactful and anointed by God for this dispensation of time; to pray healing for the broken and to speak life to every dead situation that has come as a hindrance and distraction to Christian believers. In this book, you'll find both natural and spiritual antidotes that will bring *"Healing To Your Soul."*

Pastor Ted McRae

Emerge Ministries - Miami Lakes, Florida

Elder Rhonda Ferguson-Lewis is the epitome of a godly woman full of faith who walks by faith and not by sight. She has proven herself to me to be a true friend every time I've needed her service to pray, preach, teach, conduct a women's conference, minister to my congregations, or through the ministry of prophecy. She has 'souled' herself out for the Kingdom of God in her servitude of ministering to the loss at any cost. She loves the Lord with her whole heart, soul, and mind. Elder Rhonda's monumental work, _"Soul Sessions: Volume 1 – Healing for the Soul,"_ is a testament and global perspective to your soul's need of a miraculous deliverance from the Egypt mentality and an inner cleansing of past pain. She compels you to take an assessment of your deepest soulish relationship and life's journey with God and to be intentional about being aligned and transformed by the renewal of your soul through the enlightenment of your mind to live your best life ever. This is a phenomenal read to reach your unpretentious destiny that's been determined for you before the foundation of the world. Is there anything greater than your soul? Let the healing begin!

Reverend Patricia Shuler Montgomery

Mount Zion AME Church - Santee, South Carolina

Through love, power, mercy, and grace, God divinely places His glory in clay pots. His grace is sufficient to magnify and give glory to Himself through our weaknesses. He forms our individuality and purpose through His Holy visitations and revelations until the mysteries of the Kingdom are revealed in us. It's His greatest pleasure to take us in His hands as miry clay and mold us into kings and priests! Soul Ties will enlighten you with revelation directly from the throne of God. The breath of Heaven will flow through your soul to bring a refreshingly new perspective to every area of your life. It's a gifted message from Love Himself Who reveals His treasures out of the deep places of your life experiences. That in-depth knowledge of our Creator and His will for us lifts the veil between two worlds- the dark one we've encountered, and the Kingdom of Light we find ourselves daily pressing into that brings us into the Divine Nature of our King Jesus. Soul Ties takes you on a journey through your most intimate secrets and personal experiences to get to the root of why you are where you are and why you make the decisions you make. It beautifully marries those connections to the Word of God so you can be free to live your best and blessed life now.

Dr. Kelli Vance

Empowered Ministries / Empowered Television

Barboursville, West Virginia

Preface: Soul Ties - 'The Ties that Bind'

When one speaks of SOUL TIES, they typically refer ONLY to SEXUAL ENCOUNTERS, and how these spiritual quantum entanglements tend to tie our soul to every soul we've ever had a sexual encounter with (See Volume 2). In Volume 1, through the compilations of each SOUL SESSION, you will see and understand, that whenever we are experiencing or operating in anything outside of God's character, that "something" has *attached* or **"tied"** itself to our Soul and has the ability to become the dominating influencer or controller. Paul said it best, ***"Even when I try to do good, evil is always present."*** Where is evil present? In our soul.

These *"castaways"* - demons or wicked spirits cast out of heaven with Lucifer, are always looking for a home to live in. Your soul is one of the places they choose to occupy, dwell and live. They deceitfully manipulate you to believe that how you behave, and feel is *"just who you are"* and *"how you behave, react or respond to people, circumstances and situations"* is *"just the way it is."* Even when we act out or commit to saying or doing something which is spiritually or morally questionable, we will often say, "*Well, God knows my heart...*" and yes, He does!! But can I tell you, that even your Heavenly Father says, **"The human heart is the most deceitful of all things, and desperately wicked. Who really knows how bad it is?"** Jeremiah 17:9 (NLT)

The thief (devil) comes to steal, kill and destroy. He is the father of all lies. One of his most effective lies is for you to believe that your negative and carnal behavior is OKAY. To erroneously believe that God made you that way, or to think or say, "*these are natural occurrences and they are not bothering me, so why should they bother someone else?*" is one of the biggest lies. Our behavior, whether directly or indirectly, can and will influence the behavior of others. These so-called natural inclinations are spiritual. They are the manifestation of the lying spirits that express themselves in chaos, confusion, and conflict. Where do these spirits express themselves? In Our Soul!!!

Yes, these everyday emotions, feelings and habits may be deemed natural... but you are not! You are a spiritual being able to live above these nuisances and evict them from your

Soul (*mind, will, emotions, attitudes, and intellect, etc.*). This is achieved as you ask and then allow God to break every chain (soul-tie) internally. Scripture admonishes us to ***"Work out our soul's salvation with fear and trembling"*** (Phil 2:12*)*. Why? Because at any given moment we; you and I, can be (as my grandmother would say) wrapped up, tangled up and tied up.... but unfortunately, not in the Lord. As we are made aware of these "soul-ties," we also become aware that we've been given the power to "untie" ourselves and relinquish the ownership of our soul once and forever to Jesus Christ as Savior and Lord. As your soul is untied, external changes and choices will manifest as ripe Fruit of the Spirit, enabling you to grow in the nature and character of Christ.

In Volume 1, as we seek to identify and acknowledge the "ties" that have us bound; we will realize that these ties are what have incarcerated our soul and imprisoned our thoughts, will, and emotions. A pattern that ultimately influences your mental-state, choices and actions; and can once and for all be untied. By loosing the noose, we will allow the "real me" to be FREE to be "ME." However, I Peter

1:22 says, *"we purify our soul, when we walk obediently in truth."* It is the TRUTH that we KNOW [believe intimately and obey] that truly has the power to SET us Free. Jesus already did the work, now you must do the **"works."** Faith without works is dead. Once you know the truth, you must obey the truth. That is your first and most important action step.

Are you ready to be free from emotional, mental, and behavioral soul ties? Then, I invite you to come and sit on my couch for **Volume 1 of Soul Sessions – Healing for the Soul**.

Let the Healing Begin……

Acknowledgements

I am very thankful for the support and encouragement of so many people who have supported me in my efforts to complete *Soul Sessions: Volume 1 – Healing for the Soul.* None of this would have been possible without the inspiration of the Holy Spirit, so for that I am eternally grateful to the Lord as He continues to lead, guide and direct my path.

I want to say thank you to my husband Kevin who has encouraged me to work from home for the last 8 years without complaining and always believing in the God in me from day one. Even through moments of disagreements and make ups, you have not wavered in your love and support. I Love you... "There will Never be another Love."

Thank you to each Pastor who took the time to read, review and write the foreword, commending the work God. A special thanks to Andrea A. Jordan for the design of the book cover and the final edit. We could not have completed this this work without you!

To Theresa Tippins and Stephanie Pop, thank you also for your editorial contributions.

To my sister Rhoda Ferguson Carter, who always offers a listening ear and for also being the first person to purchase my first book. Thank you for your support and being there for me and my family always.

To Jeanie Benbow Carter, my aunt, thank you for always being a source of encouragement and support by any means necessary. Thank you for volunteering to invest in the project just to be a blessing to other family members. You remain a source of inspiration.

To WOVEN, Women of Virtue Excellence & Nobility and Pearls of Wisdom – 8 years of Soul Sessions and trials and errors, good and bad, richer and poorer, sickness and health. Remember, "Just when I needed YOU" ...... You all made me desire to want to be a better woman as you all inspire and challenge me to live the life I preach about!

And to all of my family, extended family, men and women who have invited me into their homes, churches, businesses, organizations, marriages, relationships and lives... Thank you for your trust, prayers and support.

To God Be the Glory!

Introductory SOUL Session: Understanding Significant Emotional Events

We see life through what psychologists call *"colored lenses."* A person's TRUTH is very relative. In most cases, it is merely a compilation of our 'facts' derived <u>predominantly from our five senses; which are intertwined with our values, beliefs, life experiences, education, family/culture, marital status, economic status, our practicing religious or non-religious beliefs; and even defined by our country, state, city and neighborhoods we live in.</u> Each of us at any given time can encounter the same situation - and based on this "worldly system" developed from the outside but made sacred in forming our definition of the truth - we can have a different assessment of the same experience. Although in telling your truth, whatever it may be, until you see it through the eyes (mind) of Christ, you are seeing it through colored lenses.

Our life's viewpoint is also known as paradigms or mindsets; and your facts regarding your life experience can be real. The facts that you have derived from your experiences can be real. But it will still be colored or obscured based on your perception and your belief system. Until you are BORN-AGAIN, the world as you know it will predominantly influence and shape your truth from the facts. Yes, many misconstrue the facts with the truth, but it is the truth (God's word that we believe and obey) that has the transformative power to set us free. If we can't believe certain scriptures, or obey certain scriptures, then it is possible that we are not only reading and interpreting them through our colored lenses, but we are also being manipulated by a spirit of blindness. If we can't believe or trust God or obey God in certain areas of our lives, BUT BELIEVE WE ACTUALLY ARE, and cannot tell the difference; then yes, we are not only viewing Him according to our colored lenses, but we have now upgraded to being deceived by a Spirit of Blindness.

Jesus said, *"This is why I speak to them in parables: Though seeing they do not see; though hearing, they do not hear. In them the prophecy of Isaiah is fulfilled: 'You will be ever hearing but never understanding; you will be ever seeing but never perceiving....For this people's heart has grown callous; they hardly hear with their ears, and they have closed their eyes. Otherwise they might see with their eyes, hear with their ears, understand with their hearts, and turn, and I would heal them.' But blessed are your eyes because they see, and your ears because they hear. For truly I tell you, many prophets and righteous men longed to see what you see but did not see it, and to hear what you hear but did not hear it".....* Matthew 13:13-17

If we are going to respond in a godly way in every situation, we are going to need to be free from these lenses that color our judgment and can make us judgmental of ourselves, others, those in authority and even judgmental of God; simply based on how we 'SEE' things. When wearing colored lenses, we see the facts, but seldom the truth.

Our lenses or our filters, paradigm or mindsets, can become shaded or colored through our experiences, values, religious or family beliefs; culture, race, education, economic status and relationships; along with one of the most powerful influences, "words."

There is a childhood saying, *"Sticks and stones may hurt my bones, but words will never harm me."* Through the years of coaching/mentoring, the subject of 'soul wounds' would always uncover many words said that would go uncontested or unconfronted and would eventually over time shift from soul wounds to soul ties. Does any of this sound similar or familiar to you?

"You're just like your daddy."

"You're so stupid!"

"What makes you think you can do that?"

"Why can't you be more like your sister (brother)?"

"You always…. (fill in the blank)."

"You'll never succeed at that."

"No one in our family was ever like you."

"You can't do anything right."

"You're too skinny (or too fat) or dark (or light)."

"Why would anybody want to hire (or marry) someone like you?"

Well, I'm sure many of us have concluded by now, that while the broken bones will mend and heal one day, most are still waiting for the "someday" when the hurtful, poison and toxic words that pierced our soul will also mend and heal. While I know *that all things work together for my good,*" this type of healing is impossible without the Love of Christ; and yet, there are still some of "US" who are in love with Christ and still are in need of inner healing, **"Healing for the Soul."**

There will always be people in your life beginning with your parents who will either speak to your purpose or speak to your pitfall. From birth, we contend with limiting beliefs based on race, color, sex, size, shape, physical features, being the oldest, youngest or middle child, etc. But, more importantly words [that now color the way we see life], are one of the most potent tools satan uses to sabotage our future and hinder us from ever achieving our potential or fulfilling our purpose. These "words" if perceived as negative or hurtful, even from well-meaning family members, friends, leaders, and brothers/sisters in Christ;

when believed, are the things that inhibit us from living our lives to its fullest potential.

You may believe these lies about yourself due to past hurts or negative comments from people you trust, but these negative thoughts you believe about yourself, especially the ones that don't align with the truth or with what God says about you based on biblical scripture, are called **Ungodly Beliefs**.

Our belief system is built on a foundation of our beliefs, values, decisions, attitudes, agreements, judgements, expectations, vows and oaths. Our belief system affects every aspect of our life. It is reflected in our actions. It is rooted in our heart. It affects our mental, physical and spiritual health. It affects our identity and our destiny. It affects the color and the condition of our soul.

There are Godly Belief systems (GBs) and Ungodly Belief Systems (UGBs). But the truth is, ALL of us, to some extent, have wrong beliefs about ourselves, others and even God. To distinguish: Godly Belief Systems agree with God

(*His word, His nature, His character, His kingdom*). Ungodly Belief Systems are NOT.

Ungodly Beliefs (UGBs) become prominent in our way of thinking from things we've been taught, experienced, heard and/or witnessed. Ungodly Beliefs also can gain access to us through hurts and traumas in our life that I like to call, **Significant Emotional Events (SEE)**. SEEs is those traumatic and/or terrific to terrifying events that can shape our view of something or color our thoughts, reactions and actions in any given situation. It presents itself throughout our lifetime in our actions, reactions and decisions. In most cases, what you believe is a product of what you SEE in your SOUL (mind's eye) to be Your Truth. And SEEing is Believing. Proverbs 23:7 says *"For as he thinks in his heart, so he is..."*

Many of our **SEE**s has come by way of those we love, honor, and trust, mainly during our younger years leading to adulthood. Again, your teachers, coach, boy/girl scout leader, Sunday School teacher, Pastor or Spiritual leader, sorority or fraternity, mentor, and of course family members, are listed in this circle of influence. By then, our paradigm (mind-set) has been shaped and colored to believe GBs or UGBs, so much so that, "What you **S.E.E.** (and meditate on) is what you Get" ~ Good or Bad!!

There are many **S**ignificant **E**motional **E**vents that have affected how I viewed my relationships, marriage, children, friendships, society, work, church people, those in authority and even God. These events were so relevant that they also affected how I lived my life and unfortunately the poor decisions and choices I made that not only hurt me, but also those in my life. These ungodly decisions came from the influence of my UGBs (*it would take another book to share how these UGBs derived from Significant Emotional Events, that shaped the course of my life*). Thank God that ultimately my life was one day reshaped by a Godly Significant Emotional Event, when I finally surrendered it all to Jesus Christ. But, I would like to take this time before you begin the book, to share one prolific ungodly **SEEs**, which literally and spiritually was a set-up from the enemy to destroy any Godly Belief intended for me concerning money, wealth, prosperity, happiness and all that I was created to possess. Thank you for allowing me to share.

My Significant Emotional Event:

While there are many events in my life that I have had to overcome that were significant and very emotional; there were distinct experiences that shaped and molded my way of being, responding, doing and thinking throughout my adolescence leading - to a major part of my adulthood. I found out that you do not have to be tied to your past. You do not have to allow "it," whatever "it" is to define you. The end result can be freedom from these negative and painful experiences once you have a true encounter with God and a Healed Soul. I'm living my best life now- SPIRITUALLY, although not perfect, but being perfected in Him daily. When you have the mind of Christ, all things are new, including who you think YOU are!

Over the years, I have repeatedly asked for wisdom when others are included in my testimony. I've had my share of close family members (including my husband) regretting others hearing the truth that set me free but did not shine a bright or favorable light on others. This particular testimony was even closer to home and I once again turned to one of my aunts to help me SEE another 'Point-to-View'. Boy, am I glad I did!

I then allow God to speak through me and guide me in what to share and yet still show how much I care. My prayer concerning this testimony as it includes those closest to me, is that it allows the reader to know that it was more than me encountering a Significant Emotional Event and as a minister of the gospel, if what I share can help somebody, even one somebody; then I have now become a written epistle being read by men, so God can reveal what He needs to heal in others as well. This good news (the gospel) now becomes the written testimony that empowers you to know. You too can be healed TODAY from Ungodly Beliefs. I am a living witness and I do have a testimony! My statement of my truth through the years has become and remain, "My Success is NOT Negotiable..." What about yours?

So, here we go... "**Money, the root of all things evil...**" (or so I thought).

This **S**ignificant **E**motional **E**vent was set in motion between the ages of 9 and 10 years old, around fourth or fifth grade. The school year is 1968/69 and my mother and her family were experiencing their own Significant Emotional Event as they transitioned from Segregation to Integration. My mom was about 26/27 years of age, dealing with the trauma of her first divorce from my father; to become a single mother of three girls: Rhonda, Rhoda and Robin, approximately 9, 4 and 1 years of age. Adding to this S.E.E. was also having to leave her house to temporarily move back home with her parents, while also being one of the first group of African American teachers to be transferred out of her neighborhood to integrate a school populated with predominantly Caucasian and Latin students. Imagine being only 26 years of age, caught in the turmoil of these type of transitions in your life. How she coped as well as she did, I can't say or even imagine. I know her relationship with God helped...... and a whole lot of prayer.

Let me be clear. I loved my mother and I know my mother loved me and my sisters. She worked hard for her family, her church and her community. Sadly, as a young family, our lives and our relationships were at times, battered by the agonizing stress and strains of daily life, the times we grew up together in, and the various transitions we endured as women and young girls. If it truly takes a village to raise a child, then our village was an extensive one. Our values, ideals, beliefs, relationships and mindsets, were formed through this amazing extension of family members, neighbors, community, school and our home away from home, Second Baptist Church.

Second Baptist Church was 'Mecca' to our family. My grandparents took pride in being one of its founding families and were a Deacon and a Deaconess- "*A Charge to Keep I Have and a God to Glorify.*" My entire family was active. My mom being very active in the church as well, found herself a recent divorcee. This was not 'common' for our family nor the community we grew up in. While I pondered on the backstory of this S.E.E., I must also include the embarrassment this may have caused my mom and my grandparents as well.

While in the late 60s and 70s, we applauded our newfound Civil Rights. I lived with a mom, Geraldine B. Ferguson-Corbett. She had to carpool with other African American teachers approximately 40 miles round trip, 5 days a week; carrying the pride of a race and a community, while being forced to endure the burden of being the first to NOT be welcomed or feel welcomed in a new community that did not know her or welcomed her to become their child's new teacher. Yet, to this day many of her colleagues and students, (Blacks, Caucasians and Latinos) share how great and caring she was as a teacher to every child that had the pleasure of encountering her. My mom was a great person, sister, daughter, mother, teacher, friend and woman of God, but each of us when experiencing our own Significant Emotional Events can and will affect the lives of others significantly. Make no mistake about it, my mom, our community and this nation, was in the middle of an identity crisis that only time, and God would reveal and heal.

My mom and grandmother were very close. They were best friends. Keeping that in mind, this particular Significant Emotional Event which I am to share, not only was set in motion an attempt to sever our relationship as mother and daughter; but to also distort the way I viewed myself, relationships and money.

As I remember this S.E.E., I came home from playing at the park one day, and only my mother and grandmother were home. I don't know what type of day my mom had, but this day was earmarked as a day that would change the trajectory of God's original plans for my life.

Time passed, and suddenly, my mother announced that $20 went missing from her room. She said she searched around and could not find the money. Since it was just the three of us, my mother of course, blamed the missing money on me. Now, up until this point, I had never stolen anything, there was no reason for my mom not to trust me with money in the house; but in the process of elimination, she perceived and believed that I stole the money.

She repeatedly asked me what I did and where did I hide her $20. In a span of time, she continued to accuse me, but my answer remained the same, "I did not take it." I promised her I did not see it and I did not touch it. But my word was not good enough. I was accused of lying and she became very angry. She repeated that it was not her mother who took it and that it had to have been me. I began to feel guilty for something I did not do. I felt as if I was being forced to confess to something I never did, and I was in serious trouble because of it. The accusation led to me getting a very bad spanking – or beating – as we called it in those days, and throughout the beating, she continued to accuse me by saying, *"You need to admit that you stole the money; you're such a liar; and you're just like your dad."*

Let me note that those three statements – *"you're a liar,"* *"you're just like your dad,"* and *"you stole the money"* – became embedded in my subconscious and drove my decisions and actions for a large portion of my adult life.

(1) "Being a liar" was a huge one. Telling the truth did not matter so neither would telling a lie.

(2) "Being like my dad" – who was an adulterer, among other shared character gifts, talents and flaws. This statement became a living prophecy. So much so, he later committed suicide, and as my life spiraled and mirrored

these Ungodly Beliefs, for many years, I became very suicidal as well. But the Ungodly Belief I really want to hone in on from this Significant Emotional Event, was the most deeply embedded thought.

(3) "I stole money" - This incident was further fueled by anger when about a week after that event with my mother took place, I came home from school, and my grandmother asked me, *"Did Gerry tell you she found the money?"* With tears in my eyes, my answer was, *"no."* I was so hurt; but the hurt turned into anger as I remembered the beating I received, which included welts on my body, where I was struck with the belt. My grandmother went on to tell me that my mother found the money INSIDE her dresser drawer as she did not place it on top of her dresser after all. But here was the compromising promise that incarcerated my woundedness which became anger…. my grandmother then swore me to secrecy – *"don't tell her I told you,"* were her words. *"Let her tell you when she's ready."* So, for the next 30+ years I never said a word, and for the next 30+ years, pride never allowed her to tell me she found it.

Anyone who knows me would sense or even know that I am marked for greatness, but remained marginal, although I am good at anything I desire to do. In spite of my mom being unknowingly used by the enemy at that delicate age and time to implant thoughts mixed with painful emotions that derailed my future and placed me on a path of self-destruction, secrecy, and hiding the truth (lying); she always supported me and came to my rescue time and time again. However, her rescue although needed and wanted, did not come without a frequent reminder of who I was or who she thought I was like.

There was not a prophetic word I received as an adult when God did not say something to me concerning money, expansion, increase or riches. That was/is the plan that God has for me, but the enemy who comes to steal, kill and destroy, put another derailing plan in motion. Satan used the incident with my mother at that young, tender age to cause me to have a Significant Emotional Event that was so powerful that it made money an enemy, and caused a UGB to develop that would negatively influence my thoughts and actions and in return would hinder and sabotage God's plans for my life. God would use prophetic words to counter those deeply embedded demonic thoughts implanted in my wounded soul and subconscious. But, the UGBs were so strong and so believed, that even though making money came to me easily, retaining it was difficult. I would always find a way to give it away, sabotage my life with it, as well as ruin some of my closest relationships. Borrowed money seemed more comfortable or better than using or having my own. It appeared to be of some greater comfort to have someone else's money and quite an achievement to know that someone would trust me with their money. Soon borrowing money became easier than appreciating having my own. Although in the end, I devalued it and those who entrusted me with this sacred and moral responsibility.

Now, I was always a giver. The Law of Reciprocity is always at work in my life, because of my generosity, even now. But I often would repel money, reject or misuse it because it hurt me. As crazy as this may sound, this was one of the ways I could finally hurt it and pay it back for what it did to me: by abusing it like it abused me. Oh, how powerful one's thoughts and perceptions are! How powerful are our Significant Emotional Events, which lead to Ungodly Beliefs that govern and control our lives. Never mind how my misuse hurt me, in the dark recesses of my mind, I hated money and did not want any parts of it. Unbeknownst to me, money was indeed the root of evil in my life.

All my life, I was able to make money and accumulate wealth for others, but when big money came to me, it would slip out of my hands just as fast as it came. I would repel it, or I would abuse it. I would give what was mine away, just to borrow what was not mine. I would lose it, abuse it, misuse it, write bad checks, bounce checks, obtain credit cards, abuse credit cards, lose credit cards. I would spend above my means, I would lie, and I would borrow money (even when I didn't need to). I would do everything to be destructive in my own life with money – and I never knew why. Unfortunately, the one who was used by the enemy to set it all in motion, paid for it dearly due to my destructive actions. My mom always felt compelled to help me out and get me out of trouble, and deep inside I now know I even felt entitled, as I subconsciously blamed her for my problematic choices.

To this day, I remember often wondering (besides knowing she loved and cared for me), what drove her obligation. In my younger years, I used to foolishly think it was guilt, but in my latter years, I realized it was love. Listen... if you let it, the mind is a terrible thing to waste. As time passed, soon every significant relationship was challenged to the max or ruined. I even destroyed the fabric of my marriage with lying and infidelity. Then, while in the middle my own divorce, and becoming the single parent of two young children, checks were written by me again that I thought my husband would've helped me pay. So, I left them unpaid. Even though I had the money several times to pay them off, I ignorantly and stubbornly did not, as I kept giving and helping others with thousands of donations and seeds sown for spiritual and personal purposes. Even when the vendor reached out to me personally, I ignored him because I was angry and just did not care anymore. It would appear that all that was said about me came true, so what did it matter?!! The only thing that kept me on this side with the living were my children. But like my dad, the pressures built up to a place that death seemed like a much-needed relief, as it became a desired way to escape from it all.

Eventually, a complaint was made that lead to it becoming a police investigation. Yes, I was identified as a Police Officer (also my dad's lifelong occupation) because I wrote the checks while in uniform. At the conclusion of the investigation, I was suspended without pay and ordered to pay the vendor, which I did. This internal investigation, which was closed, obviously was not over. This closed case was selected by the State Attorney's Office for further investigation. A few months earlier, a new office was established whose sole purpose was to investigate the misconduct of law enforcement officers. My case became #002, the second case investigated. An entire year later after the initial incident, and seven months after the checks and fines were repaid, the ASA in charge decided to press felony charges (the checks were over $200, which is a felony in the State of Florida). The ASA also added another charge called "Defrauding an Innkeeper". WHAT???? Are you now accusing me of going to the store with the **intent** to STEAL these items from the owner?

Did I blame and was I angry with the State Attorney Office and with the Police Department? YES!!! This two-year ordeal only strengthened the same emotional 'Soul Tie' by adding another similar incident to my Significant Emotional Event. Here I am again, getting prosecuted for something already paid off, settled by law, and the internal police case closed over a year ago. But, to add insult to injury, I am also being accused of intentionally stealing once again.

Soon after the charges were made official, a warrant was issued, and I was arrested. Fast-forwarding to a year and four months later, our court date was set. By then, my husband and I were engaged in marriage counseling, and as the charges were dropped, so was I as a Police Officer.

Of course, I felt unjustly treated. Of course, I had rights. Of course, I wanted to sue (*but I was told God would vindicate... and, seven years later he did - with interest*). Yet, during that time, can you imagine how **angry** I was again...... AT MONEY!!!

Over time I knew something was wrong. I can be fooled and even can be a little slow at times, but I catch on eventually. So, I looked to counseling and pastoral guidance to begin to unwrap the years and layers of my love-hate relationship with money and my life. I did better, but I was still bitter, hurt, embarrassed and without a job, home and a husband (SEE the patterned). I felt like I was robbed, as I began to discover that the underlying reason that I repelled money was as a result of this Significant Emotional Event that no one ever told me about (I THOUGHT) or acknowledged as real. Instead, I WAS STILL BEING JUDGED FOR MY ACTIONS and the true causation was never discussed or dealt with spiritually or emotionally. Although now, I must admit, I can recall many times when my Spiritual Father would say, *"Rhonda, you need to be healed."* It was indeed a heart issue, but I always looked at the obvious; the symptoms, and not the cause. Not one time, did I ever think the root of it all began with this Significant Emotional Event!

I soon went outside of the church to seek help through therapy. I was diagnosed by a Christian psychologist with OCD - Obsessive Compulsive Disorder. Okay... I can see that as a behavior pattern, too. BUT, where did it come from? What is the root? What is causing me to behave this way? Why can't I truly change? These were questions I agonized over and over in my mind. For years I had massive migraines and now needed to take strong medication which made me sleep. I became depressed and began to escape by taking the same medication even when I was not experiencing a migraine headache, or I would take over-the-counter sleep-aids. As long as I was asleep, I did not have to face anything or anybody or feel depressed and worthless. When awake, the work it took to try to 'make-up" for the deficiencies in character, became too hard. Soon I perfected the art of becoming a man-pleaser and continued to use my gifts, skills and talents to deflect and distract others, as life went on.

During my struggle to try to do and be better, I felt I was not spiritual enough and did not really believe God enough, or that He even loved me enough. SERIOUSLY, that "*Victim Mentality*" is a soul killer! I received Words of Prophecy from so many. Prophetic proclamations, that constantly spoke to the potential, purpose and plans God had for my life. I would also release these same type words that brought hope to so many; but I myself was suffocating on the inside without an oxygen tank. To add to my woundedness, as an adult, I heard more word bashings similar or like the ones I heard as a child. These words that reinforced UGBs of myself resonated deep in my soul and now drove my thoughts, words and actions, as if I had no choice.

These offensive words, told to me by well-meaning people that were influential in my life, would soon come to be what I describe in Soul Sessions as, simply the 'facts'. Statements like, "*Rhonda, but you've hurt so many people;*" "*You're not a real woman of integrity;*" "*You've done a lot of damage to others;*" and my favorite, "*God can't trust you.*" My response in my head and heart was, and "*rightfully so...*" "*why should He?*" All of this seemed so true. Others obviously believed it too or why would they say it? But, thank God, it was not the truth about the real me. Those reinforced statements only acknowledged and focused ON THE FACTS of my life, which were a result of my UGBs in action!!

Needless to say, years later, one Thanksgiving when my mom moved to Georgia, my family and I went to visit her. My son Kaleb went into the back area of the house to use the restroom for a few minutes. My mother later came out and said someone went in her room and stole something. She began to accuse Kaleb. Up until that moment, I had never known Kaleb to steal anything or to even lie about something as significant as that. He respected and loved my mom more than anything, but when she accused him, I could see, he was in the middle of his own Significant Emotional Event. When I saw this same spirit trying to damage and wound my son's soul through a false accusation, I lost my cool and spoke to my mom in a way I never had. I had never raised my voice to her in that way, but generationally, what was happening was this same spirit trying to attack my son now in the same mode and methodology, by accusing him of stealing. Grandmother was no longer with us, so it was in that moment I felt **FREE** to tell my mom what was told to me, that transpired years ago concerning those $20. Those SAME $20, that I received a 'beating' for NOT stealing all those years ago. After, I finally said all I felt I needed to say and calmed down, the conversation went something like this:

Mom: "Well why didn't you say something back then?"

Me: "Why didn't you say something? You found the money you beat me for and never told me that you found it, and I should've said something to you? Momma you were wrong then. Could it be you are wrong now? Here you are now accusing Kaleb of the same thing. Is that fair? Is that right? Did you check correctly? Because you found the money in the past, could it be that you misplaced it again?"

Mom: "Well, I looked everywhere." And anyway, what you're speaking of is in the past. You're grown now.

Me: I know I'm grown. And I tried to move on, but obviously as I grew it must have grown with me, because I held it in me, after being told not to say nothing to you.

Silence... (Still no apology) ...... I walked away.

Her husband proceeded to get up and look, he didn't see it either. BUT.... eventually, she found it and this time it was different. My mom apologized to my son Kaleb, and then she apologized to me. It was during this time my mom was being challenged with sickness and I did not want to add to her challenge, but I was still angry, even after the apology.

I thought her apology was what I needed to hear and what I waited and longed for, but it still did not appear to be enough. God did allow this incident to occur once again, for us to get it right and to break the cycle of this Significant Emotional Event, and for that I was grateful.

I, of course, apologized to my mother as well because I had never spoken to her in that tone. Thirty plus years had gone by with me hurting and punishing myself as I held onto a secret about a lie of something that hurt me tremendously, just to protect someone else. I WAS ANGRY! That experience and secret lying dormant within my wounded soul became a strong soul tie, that caused me to spend years punishing myself and hurting and disappointing others. This **SEE** became a yoke that drove my ungodly decisions and actions for years. It was not until my 8th year of attending a God Encounter Conference that God revealed what He wanted to heal in me.

When the student is truly ready, the teacher (Holy Spirit) appears. I found myself in another major transition and it was during this time someone asked me to mentor them. I thought, "Who Me?" I remember telling God the many reasons why I was disqualified (sort of like Moses). I had been a police officer, teacher, ordained minister, certified counselor, life coach, trainer, speaker and leader for other companies and in the church for years, and yet still felt like a failure. But this question would not go away. To now step out as minister and a Spiritual Coach in the marketplace (outside of the church structure), to help others who saw something good and godly in me, was surreal.

One day I was rehearsing to God, how all other personal life coaches and mentors had "stuff" to show and to offer and how I had nothing. At this time, we were losing everything of value due to the past mishandling, disunity and poor stewardship and taxes. Sure, I can preach, coach and teach, but mentoring was something totally different. I did NOT feel qualified and yet, God allowed it anyway!! I remember saying, *"God I have nothing to offer or give these ladies."* His answer, *"That's good. All I want you to give them is me. You lift me up Rhonda and I will draw."* For the past eight years, God has been faithful, and He has done just that. I don't advertise this mentoring group called WOVEN, "Women Of Virtue Excellence & Nobility" ... I kept my promise and God has kept His. He draws! Each one reaches one, and what a joy it has been as we all heal and grow stronger and wiser in the Lord together.

These ladies often share how I helped and saved their lives. I ALWAYS remind them how they helped to SAVE my life. In my mentoring them, I could not teach or impart what I was not and what I was unable to overcome. So, I had to really work on my Soul Salvation with fear and trembling. For the sake of their souls, my Soul became a priority.

This did not come without trial and error, and for the first few years I went in the strength of my gift and most of the time in what I was taught instead of what was actually caught. But God still used me until I was tired of being used by me. I can remember many nights crying out for TRUE change. I knew I was gifted, but all I wanted was God to be pleased. One day my man-pleasing turned to God-pleasing. I can't tell you the exact moment, but I remember when it did. I was on the road to healing and recovery. Everything the enemy stole God was reconciling me unto himself and then to others. Some of the relationships that I truly made a mess of God began to restore as He taught me how to begin to totally depend on Him and no longer look to others.

There were so many bad monetary decisions I made over the years, that it was a huge challenge to go back and correct it all. What I was unable to do, however, with God's help and my desire to do the right things and move forward, my small actions became progressively successful. There were some people that forgave me and forgave the debt, as I (we) lost our job, our cars, properties we owned, our money (taxes), my health was tremendously challenged, and I also lost my mom. As time passed, I became a schoolteacher (my mom's career) and taught criminal justice and law (even with a felony record). This allowed me to reconcile myself to my past and parties I directly and indirectly blamed for my life choices and reckless behaviors and destructive actions. After my four-year commitment concluded with the school board, I decided to step out in faith and began coaching and mentoring full time. It was a bold move. But one I have never regretted. To be able to look ahead, and change my way of being, doing and thinking as it pertains to many things was/is so satisfactory. I made amends where I was able to make amends. I adjusted where I was able to adjust. But eventually we still lost our home and had to relocate. In all transparency, to date, there are still two major debts I need to repay, but I thank God for the light at the end of the tunnel. I wish I had a fairytale ending for you, but I, too, am still working on my soul salvation daily, but now with true fear and trembling. I choose to please God and not man. I pray at the end of your Soul Sessions you will too. As I continue to do what is right, my goal and prayer is to be 'debt' free ~ and owe no man nothing but love!!!

Another thought I had to reconcile was why did grandmother tell me not to say anything to my mom about her finding the twenty dollars she said I stole. I really was stuck on why I was told to lie. I felt it helped shaped my way of thinking and how I felt about the truth. One day after prayer while half-asleep, I felt I was back in that moment of time in my grandmother's house. God began to open my eyes and my heart to realize that my grandmother was keenly aware of what was at stake for my mom. She knew of all the transitions and trauma my mom was experiencing and being forced upon her as a 26-year-old divorcee with three little girls. She knew my mom was dealing with grief and "loss". But she could not stop to heal. To stop would mean to quit, and Benbow women do not quit! She lost her husband. She lost her home. She lost her community (as she began to travel to another foreign one to teach in daily). She lost friends and co-workers and I'm sure she felt alone and lost as well. When she "lost" her $20, being able to blame someone for the 'losses' was almost long overdue. Now, like I said earlier, my grandmother and my mom were very close, best friends. Like any good mom, what she desired to do was to protect her baby girl (even though grown), from any additional hurt, embarrassment, shame, guilt or loss of respect from her daughter. As I thought back to that day in Georgia, I remembered how shock and then hurt the expression on my mom face looked when I told her that I knew. I knew by the look on her face, that she wished I never knew. Two people. Same incident. Different outcomes. But, one Significant Emotional Event.

Note: *This entire Significant Emotional Event involving three generations, was a setup to alter my future. God did not design it, but He did allow it. Why? For such a time as this! Now it was time to break every chain and "Soul Tie" for our generations to come!*

As time passed, God began to show me what ungodly spirits affected so many areas of my life for all those years. When I returned home that year after attending the God Encounter, we relocated to South Carolina. It was in this place that I spent time alone with God daily and began to adjust how I viewed and what I thought and believed concerning money. Even though my husband and I were at a point that we lost literally everything, and was living in someone else's home, I was determined to do what I could to make amends with others. I had faith I could do it, but the works went back and forth at first. The fear of being confronted for my wrong was overwhelming. Not only fear, but there was a tie around my soul that really was still trying to protect my reputation. Sometimes we feel avoidance will make things go away. That spirit of denial and pride only gets stronger not weaker, the more you *"leave it alone"*. One day, God told me, *"Confrontation leads to Mediation, which leads to Reconciliation. But it all begins with the conversation. Go, make the calls. Talk to others. My favor is upon you and I am with you."* **This** has been and is still my journey. Every day I unravel another tie that had me bound. But it is the TRUTH that SETS me FREE!

In essence, these Significant Emotional Events (SEE), or as they have been termed, can derail your life, sabotage your life, and hinder you from being and doing all that God has called, anointed and appointed you to be and do. They can appear innocent or they can be intentional but make no mistake; they are on a mission to not only sabotage your life, but they are also created to kill, steal and destroy your thoughts, your future, and the significant relationships in your life. Over the years I have lost valuable relationships and there are even family members that are still upset with me about the lie I told and the money I borrowed but did not pay back. Thank God we overcome by the blood of the Lamb and the word of our testimony. This is once again an overcoming moment for me, and I hope and pray it will be for you, too. While we may be ignorant to the devices of the enemy to kill, steal and destroy; our ignorance , not negate his ability to manipulate us through the significance of every one of life's emotional events, and it will not negate the opportunities you will have to go and get things in divine order. We, too, have a charge to keep and a God to glorify.

It is vital and necessary to identify every S.E.E. and every Ungodly Belief. We have to work through them in the Word by Faith after we have commanded the spirit of blindness, rejection, self-deception, and offense to leave our very souls, and whenever possible don't forget the works. Wherever they are; pray, locate, reach out to the ones you've hurt along your journey and do your part to reconcile the offense.

One of the very first things I require that each person being coached or mentored by me do is to complete [with total transparency] is a *Soul Session Deliverance Questionnaire* that was created. They also are required to attend our **God Encounter** for inner healing. It is imperative to know the nature of the battle in each of us. It is then my mandate to lead them away from the facts (UGBs), and then toward the truth that shall set them free (GBs).

In this **Soul Session Volume 1**, we have unfolded the Word of God, added wisdom to assist with your understanding, and mixed this with practical and spiritual action steps, as well as overcoming testimonies. I truly believe that this method that God has given us will assist in your road to being free from all emotional, familiar and mental soul ties. In Volume 2 – is where we will focus on Sexual Soul Ties.

I invite you to join me by stepping into the Pool of Bethesda. The waters are being stirred. This is one place where we all can still be healed and set free through the pages of this book.

In addition, you will be provided with some exercises that will assist you in SEEing these Significant Emotional Events for what they are. You will also be given a specific prayer, suggested scripture and a particular topical song to listen to as you allow God to reveal all that He desires to heal. The prophetic words and prayers are to also empower you to supersede any past SEEs and UGBs with hope and a future; as you experience and encounter God's love and healing virtue in your very own Soul Session. It's time to break free of every soul tie. It's time for Healing for the Soul.

I Believe and therefore, I Speak. And it is So. Manifest!

Rhonda F. Lewis

TABLE OF CONTENTS

Foreword
Preface – Soul Ties – 'The Ties that Bind'
Introduction – Understanding Significant Emotional Events
Soul Session #1 – Prophetic Insight and Wisdom
Soul Session #2 – Lord, Help My Unbelief *(Unbelieving Believers)*
Soul Session #3 – Commanding My Soul *(Spirit of Discouragement)*
Soul Session #4 – Dishonesty is NOT the Best Policy *(Lying Spirits)*
Soul Session #5 – Forgive and You Will Be Forgiven *(Spirit of Unforgiveness)*
Soul Session #6 – I Think Myself Happy – Defeating Unhappiness *(Spirit of Despair and Oppression)*
Soul Session #7 – Rejecting Rejection *(Spirit of Rejection)*
>   **Part 1** – Performance Oriented and Driven
>   **Part 2** – Fixers
>   **Part 3** – Self-Rejection
>   **Part 4** – Misplaced Identity - *(The Root of Rejection)*
Soul Session #8 – To Be or NOT to Be *(Spirit of Indecisiveness)*
Soul Session #9 – Breaking Ungodly Beliefs and Unhealthy Soul Ties *(Prayers of Renunciation)*
Soul Session #10 – What's in Your Hand? *(Spirit of Faith)*
Daily Soul Session Declarative Prayer

Soul Session #1: Prophetic Insight and Wisdom

WARNING! Heal Soul Wounds before they Become Soul Ties!

The Lord is highlighting soul wounds. If you have experienced a deep wound, trauma, or betrayal, it can only be healed by allowing the wound to be cleaned, disinfected, and then closed. This must take place, or the wounded soul will never heal properly. We need to let God clean us out and close our wounds. We can no longer cover it up or place a band-aid on an open wound. There are gaping holes in our souls; open wounds that the enemy can and will continually operate in; bringing affliction to your soul and body. **The enemy uses these covered up open wounds against you. But God desires to reveal what He wants to heal. His desire is for you to not only be healed, but also be made whole: Spirit, Body and Soul.**

This will be different, and even look different, for each individual person. At times, God will assign someone to your life that knows how to help bring you the right healing for the type of wound needing treatment. Look at this like a special doctor that is called in for specific injuries. In some instances, He will move you geographically to a new area, a new job, a new church, or connect you to new relationships. He will use these persons, places and things to bring more awareness to what you are doing or not doing to mask the open wound. Sometimes, it has been just God and I coming together to close one of my wounds by confessing my faults and my sin. In other instances, cleansing not only came from confessing, but through forgiveness of others, forgiving myself, and yes... even forgiving God. Some of us blame God for our life's challenges and soul ties to past incidents, accidents and people. Either way, many times, to heal from a wounded spirit begins with admissions, confessions and inevitably - forgiveness.

**~ God knows what it will take to see you whole.
Let it happen. ~**

God really knows how best to do it. For me, healing has been a journey filled with a variety of moments and ways in which He chose to do it. At times, it felt like He was using a bristle brush to scrub out the debris that had collected in my open wound. There were even times He placed others in my life who became that brush or even a warm blanket where I simply felt loved and safe from what I perceived was harming me. Those were the times I had to open up and admit my wrong and allow others assigned to my life, to do what I knew God had sent them to do- to help my wounds heal properly. **Had I avoided these divine appointments (which to be honest I had on previous occasions), I would have allowed infection to set in and contaminate my soul and spread to different parts of my body, sometimes even until they manifested physically** [i.e... stress, high blood pressure, sleeplessness, headaches, back pain, chest pains, arthritis...].

So many times, we like to think we are fine, but we are really just numb, in denial, going through the motions, faking it until we make it, and avoiding the pain of healing at any and all cost. Here's the thing...

~ If you don't deal with your soul wounds; they will deal with you as a soul tie! ~

Soul ties will begin to affect other parts of your life. You will begin to make choices and decisions for your life out of those wounds. Those soul wounds become a filter that works against what the Spirit of God is doing as He lives in your human spirit. Soul wounds can clog you up like a dam in a river. For many of you, this is a matter of feeling your feelings; or getting into those places with God, and allowing Him to remove those barriers and obstacles, so you can experience the power of His presence in your life in an even greater measure. When those blocks are removed, the flow of His Spirit will increase as it moves more freely throughout your entire being. Let that thought encourage you to embrace the pain of dealing with soul wounds before they become soul ties. The Lord reminded me when I was dealing with some soul wounds of my own, that the pain of regret for not facing those things is far greater than the pain of facing them and going through them with Him, in order to be made whole. Trust me, it's worth it!

~ Many times, we think we are being led fully by our spirit, but in reality, we are being led by our soul wounds. ~

Ladies and Lords – You can do this! You can be made whole. Whatever or whoever has fractured or wounded your soul; it's time to Let Go and Let God. Cast all of your cares, hurts, pains, wounds, on Him, because He cared enough to take it all to the cross and nailed it there. He died so that you can live, and live life without the wounds and weights that have so easily sabotaged and negatively affected your life. Face yourself and take the road to healing that the Lord has laid before you. Receive this Word from the Lord below and stay the course! I have already prayed for you, that your faith fails not!

Prophetic Release and Declaration:

"I am cleaning you out in a massive way. Up until this time in your life, your emotions, your spirit, and all that you are, were influenced by soul wounds that you have allowed to become emotionally charged soul ties. Allowing the roots to these wounds to be ripped out can change your perception to see Me, to see your circumstances, more rightly. Your emotions have been up and down because I am refashioning so much in you internally. You are being re-established and reintegrated. Trust the process and

remain in My rest, so that I may finish the work I have started in you. You will now be led by your spirit as never before. You will be sharper, quicker, and less resistant to the leading of My Spirit, because the enemy is losing his ground in you to war against My plans and purposes for your life. This is going to become more apparent to you as you walk out the new you in the days to come. Spread your wings. Stay close to Me now; closer than ever before. Hunger and thirst after My righteousness. Stay submitted to the process you are in. This is key during your transition. Be obedient to the process. As you read this road map, take ownership of what you have allowed to occur. Be accountable for your inability to heal yourself without me and others I will send to you. Forgive, and now let it go. I have greater things ahead planned for you. You are coming out as you take each step forward under My power and direction. It's time. If you stay submitted to My way of bringing this all together for you, it will unfold with ease and this Soul Session will be simply a sense of adventure moving you spiritually and systematically from bondage to true freedom in me," says the Lord.

And it is So! Manifest!

Soul Session #2: Lord, Help My Unbelief

(Unbelieving Believers)

Recently, God directed me to tell a group of people just how much He believed in them. As God impressed this on my heart, I questioned it because it sounded so obvious, so simple. But over the weeks that followed, God took me on a journey to teach me that I actually had no idea just how much He believes in me, too. Although, it was good and accurate information, God said I had to understand the depth within this seemingly simple truth before I could share it again with anyone else.

Do you know how much God believes in you? He believes in you absolutely. He believes in your potential and ability. He believes that you are perfectly equipped to do all He has destined for your life. Why? Because everything you are is who He created you to be!

God created you in His own *"image and likeness."* He deliberately gave you His DNA, with the intent in creating you to be like Him. He then believed in mankind so much that He gave you and me authority and dominion over every other living creature on the planet. This is how much the Almighty God believes in you and what you are capable of doing.

These are awesome truths known by most Christians, but for many the realization of what they are reading, and hearing has not hit home in their souls/hearts, even though they may think they understand it in their mind/heads. We say it with our mouths, but the truth is far from us. How do I know this to be a fact? By observing and interacting daily with many people and Christians who live their lives as victims rather than victors. We are a people made in God's image; with a dominion mandate. You see, knowing the scripture is not enough. You need to really believe them and be able to work the word in your own life, at any place, on any given day, at anytime and anywhere in your world. NOT JUST IN A CHURCH BUILDING OR CHURCH SERVICE! The truth is: YOU ARE THE CHURCH!!!

The problem we have in our worship centers, or "the church" today, is that we have lots of believers who are actually unbelievers. There is an epidemic of **unbelieving believers**. A 'Believer' is not just a term used to describe people who believe in Christ, it is a term that should characterize how we live our lives now, and for the rest of our lives~ by Faith! Knowing that nothing is impossible is one thing. BELIEVING nothing is Impossible is the real thing! Believers not only need to believe the word of God, but we really must believe in God who is the Word. When we believe in God and what His word says – by faith – we will believe what He says about us personally, our destiny, our future and our purpose in life.

Today, ask yourself and honestly assess your response: Do you really believe God loves and believes in you, no matter what? Regardless of your past or past mistakes and regardless of what you may have said and done – Do you really believe that the promises in the Bible apply to you? Do you really believe that you are called? Do you believe that in you is the power and ability to heal the sick, meet people's needs, live prosperously, and make a difference? If you answered no or maybe or even pondered for a moment to any of these questions; could you be an unbelieving believer?

Is it really possible to be close to God, to be in his House (church-building) three to four times a week, to attend seminary or Bible College, raise your hands in worship, feel the presence of God, quote scriptures and yet still be an unbelieving believer? Duh......Yes!! Even Jesus' disciples struggled with this issue. You would read where He would say from time to time, *"O' Ye of little faith!"*

Jesus gave them authority to heal the sick and cast out demons; which they went out and did. Yet only a few chapters later, faced with a similar situation; we find them in fear and confusion and due to doubt, negativity and their unbelief, it renders them ineffective against the enemy. Please note: at one-point Jesus himself then expressed His disappointment when he called those that followed Him an *"unbelieving and perverse generation"* (Reference Mat 17:17 & Luke 9:41).

Now, the disciples were close to Jesus; they lived and traveled with Him, had been chosen by Him, and saw Him perform many miracles, and yet, they still had unbelief in their hearts. We read that they were *"unbelieving believers"* in so many situations they faced. This is why I do not assume for one minute that we who even have Holy Spirit living within us now, have mastered our surrender to trusting and believing God. It is an ever-increasing process with each encounter! If the closeness of the disciples to Jesus didn't eradicate some of their unbelief, how much more must we "the church" remain aware of this potentiality to operate as unbelieving believers? As we praise, worship, work, function and make ungodly choices daily this IS EVIDENT. During this chapter, this is the moment in the uncovering the discovery of realizing as I did when I myself cried out, *"Lord, help me overcome my unbelief!"* (Mark 9:24)

So, you may say: Rhonda, how do you know if you are a believing believer? Well, very simple…. By what you do!!! Believers are not only hearers or reciters of the Word; they are doers of the Word. Belief is a powerful motivator; it is a force that energizes people to do something. Belief is the conviction of thought the leads to faith in action. It's the word and your thoughts at work!!

Take Gideon, for example. He thought he was the weakest of the weak when God came and called him a "mighty warrior!" God was just expressing who he really was and just how much He believed in him. His next command was then, *"Go in the strength you have and save Israel"* regardless of what he thought originally, belief energized him into action. (Reference Judges 6:12, 14)

Moses' first response to God's command to go and deliver Israel from Egypt was, "I can't do it." But as God affirmed, "I believe that you can do this," Moses began to believe, and this motivated him to action. God didn't spend a long-time reassuring Moses because if God says you can do it, He expects you to believe it too. Your questioning suggests that God's belief in you is misplaced, but God knows you better than you know yourself; He knows you can do it!

God spoke to Noah and effectively said, *"I believe in you and my favor is on your life. Now I want you to go and build me an ark because I am going to send rain to flood the earth."* Noah had never seen rain before and had no idea what an ark was, but he still went and built one. God's expression of belief in him motivated him to extraordinary action.

All these men accomplished incredible things from just one word or one encounter with God. They had a revelation of just how much God believed in them, and it went so deep into their hearts/minds (thoughts) that they came away from their encounter hearing "nothing is impossible" and believing it enough to try the impossible. This same God has got some amazing things for you to do too. However, you will never accomplish them unless you take God seriously and believe Him when He says He wants to use you. God takes the appearance of ordinary just to prove to others and yourself just how extraordinary you supernaturally are! You are the original Superman(woman) and just don't know it yet. So, what do you do? You act like you're Clark Kent instead.

So, **"What good is it my brothers if someone claims to have faith but has no deeds?" said the Apostle James. Faith** *always has a corresponding action. Do you believe that you are to love your enemies? Where then is your corresponding behavior? Do you believe that you are salt of the earth and light to the world? Where then is your involvement in a darkened society? Do you believe you are healed? Where then are your words and actions that continue to call those facts (symptoms) a lie and command the truth to be revealed? Never say that you believe God if you are not expressing it in action; to do so is self-deception and it doesn't fool God or anyone else in the long run"* (James 2).

You see, belief gets you out of the boat!

One night as the disciples were crossing Lake Galilee, the weather turned stormy. Then: *"Shortly before dawn Jesus went out to them, walking on the lake. When the disciples saw him walking on the lake, they were terrified. 'It's a ghost,' they said, and cried out in fear. But Jesus immediately said to them: 'Take courage! It is I. Don't be afraid.' 'Lord, if it's you,' Peter replied, 'tell me to come to you on the water.' 'Come,' he said. Then Peter got down*

out of the boat, walked on the water and came toward
Jesus. But when he saw the wind, he was afraid and,
beginning to sink, cried out, 'Lord, save me!'" (Matthew
14:25-30).

The reaction of the disciples that night illustrates four
positions we can find ourselves in when it comes to
believing God:

1. The Terrified Believer (spirit of fear)

If you are in the boat (church), then like the disciples
(members), you love God or at least enjoy being in His
presence and/or in the company of other churchgoers. You
may be saved, or you just consider yourself not a bad
person. In the boat you have found a safe place and you
intend staying there. You don't like waves and commotion.
Then suddenly, as with the disciples; a voice starts
challenging where you are. It says, "You can do more, be
more and experience more than this." God is calling you to
a new level, but you identify with the terrified disciples in
the boat. You operate in fear. You don't like confrontation.
You don't really like change. You even pray for peace out of

fear. You're one of those believers that won't do certain things God has called or assigned you to do because you don't want the backlash. You won't pray for patience because you fear going through something to get it!! Do you know who you are?

Getting out of the boat can be frightening. Getting out of the boat [BS1] means embracing the unknown, and action can test your essential belief system. The challenge is: Do you believe that the God of your boat is also the God of the unknown ocean? Do you believe that this same God controls the wind, the waves and the sea? You may be scared of moving on or stepping out, but all that hinders you is deciding whether or not you really believe God when He says "come" or not. God has not given you the spirit of fear, but of love, power, and a sound mind. Listen, this is one of my favorite quotes stated by former President of South Africa, Nelson Mandela, on the day of his inauguration:

"*Our deepest fear is not that we are inadequate. Our deepest fear is that we are powerful beyond measure. It is our light, not our darkness that most frightens us. We ask ourselves, who am I to be brilliant, gorgeous, talented and*

fabulous? Actually, who are you not to be? Your playing small doesn't serve the world. There's nothing enlightened about shrinking so that other people won't feel insecure around you. We are meant to shine, as children do....and as we let our own light shine, we unconsciously give other people permission to do the same. As we are liberated from our own fear, our presence automatically liberates others."
Marianne Williamson

2. The Inquisitive Believer (spirit of procrastination/doubt)

You may be in the boat, and like Peter you immediately recognize God's voice. Even though you are scared, you are inquisitive. Though surrounded by people who refuse to get out of the boat, your heart is pounding, and you know you have to do something about it. Like Peter, your response is, "if this is you, tell me to come!" You are one who needs one sign... then two signs... you feel the need to pray and keep on praying. It's called procrastination, BUT NOW...Jesus answered with one word, "Come." He didn't explain how to come or what to do, it is simply a test of your belief.

If you know that God has asked you to do something, then stop hanging around with the terrified unbelievers in the boat and change your environment by stepping out. Jesus said that you must deny yourself, pick up your own cross, and follow HIM. If your momma doesn't go, if your spouse won't get out of the boat, if your best friend doesn't want to change…. Be inquisitive enough to have faith in God! Be inquisitive enough to go far enough to know that He is God, and besides Him there is no other, and no other way. God is now telling you to come. Today He is saying, come up to your potential, come up to the level I have called you, come to a place called destiny, come. Come today, I bid you to come and step into greatness. *"For I know the plans I have for you,"* says the Lord. *"Plans of peace and not evil to bring you to an expected end…"* Come!!

3. The Indecisive Believer (spirit of indecision)

Some of you are hearing this and thinking, *"I've already got out of the boat."* You are one who decided, went for it and now you are walking on water. In having decided to move forward into what God told you, doubts are now creeping in. The waves of circumstance and disappointment are crashing around you, and you wonder whether it was a mistake to step out of the boat.

Was it a mistake to leave this job?

Go back to school?

Start this business?

Leave this relationship?

Buy this house?

Get married or leave a relationship?

The list of endless questions can go on, but ultimately, *"A double-minded man is unstable in all of his ways."* Not just some of his ways... ALL! He will not accomplish anything.

To you God is saying, *"Don't look at the waves, believe!"* God hasn't changed His mind; He still believes in you. It's just a storm, and His belief in you is stronger than any adversity you will face, so keep going. *Trust in the Lord with all your heart and lean not to your own understanding in ALL your ways acknowledge Him and He will direct your path.*

Never let adverse circumstances alone determine whether you should continue, or not. Jesus promised His disciples that "in this world you will have trouble." Your belief should strengthen with every storm you face because fundamentally you are convinced that in Christ you have "overcome the world" and your destiny is secure in His hands.

4. The Sinking Believer (spirit of doubt)

Now, to all of you who feel like you are sinking fast, I'd say two things: First, well done for getting this far. Second, get back up and believe again! Remember why and what got you out of the boat in the first place. Ask yourself; what's changed? God has not!! God is still in control. He still believes in you and is still calling you. God has need of you! To the sinking Peter, Jesus reached out a hand and caught him. To you He also says, "I'm here, why did you doubt?" Doubt will sink your life every time so let any doubt be drowned out by your strong belief.

Remember - if you are the one who stepped out on the water, then like Peter, while the other disciples were afraid and stayed in the boat, you heard the voice of God and responded. You got out the boat first and decided to become the **first to follow** Jesus. Say, *"I am a first follower and not an unbelieving believer!"* Then, say to yourself, *"No turning back. I won't go back. I just don't believe He brought me this far to leave me. He is a very present help in the time of trouble or need. He promised to never leave me nor forsake me. So, this too shall pass."* Believe me when I say (singing), *"Oh, the sun will come out tomorrow."* Yes, the Sun (SON) is shining even though it may seem dark. Even when the waters seem rough. Tell yourself, *"No matter what, I'm going to ride with the rhythm of the waves and let the force of this wind propel me to my destination. I shall not be stopped."* Ain't no stoppin' me now, I'm on the move in Jesus!

With that being said, no matter if you are in believer status 1, 2, 3 or 4, though challenges may arise, you must remember: Peter's belief in God meant he was the only disciple who ever knew what it was like to walk on water. Like him, first followers have some great experiences. First followers are always the ones who do what God has said first. They launch the initiative; they write the song or the book and start a business or a ministry. This is because they have a revelation of just how much God believes in them. His belief energizes them, and in return, first followers energize the world. Gideon, Moses, Noah and Peter were all first followers. They understood that believing and doing couldn't be separated. Today we need an army of believers who are all "first followers".

Never allow your life to be manipulated by unbelieving believers; by those who will never get in or out of the boat. Their soul is anchored or tied to the spirit of fear, indecisiveness, doubt and unbelief. These are friends and family, who, every time you even mention stepping out to do something for God, are quick to express their concerns cloaked as "wise counsel and experience." Tell them you're going to the other side, and instead, yoke your life to believing believers whose souls are anchored in the Lord. These are those who may see the problems, but their belief in the promise silences all fear, doubt or unbelief.

In addition, something you may want to avoid when the storms of life come is being yoked in the boat with those unequally yoked. Though normally used to describe relationships between Christian and non-Christians, I believe this scripture has a wider wisdom to pass on in our present context. If there are unbelieving believers out there, you should not be yoked with them either - especially in a crisis! In fact, some unbelieving believers will do more damage to your walk with God and trust in God, than a sinner or non-believer ever could. This type of relationship is far more subtle and pervasive. It has proven to be more deadly and hindering for you to be in a relationship of any sort (romantic, business, or relational), with a carnal Christian. Eventually the believer, if not resolute, will succumb to the subtleness of compromise. It evidences itself in seemingly innocent questions, such as:

"Did the Bible really say it that way?"

"Did God really mean that?"

"Come on, who is it going to hurt?"

"God knows your heart."

"Why not just have fun every now and again? Everybody else is doing it."

"Grace covers it all, so why not?"

"The bible was written a long time ago, most of this stuff does not even apply to today's believer..."

Have you heard any of them? If so, then, "RUN FORREST RUN!!!" (Forrest Gump 1994)

If your response or comment, is not biblically based, when faced with these objections to doing what's right and biblical, the words not become destructive seeds that will cause and allow your belief to settle, agree and compromise with what was just sown. It is at that very moment, you are now walking on water in your boat without a paddle, and the waves crashing against your boat present themselves as doubt, indecisiveness, unbelief, carnality, complacency, man-pleasing, and the willingness to compromise.

Compromising is a poisonous fruit. It is the seed of unbelief that will germinate, grow and bring forth fruit after its own kind. It is the anchor someone just threw in the middle of your boat. Do you see the hole? If you are tied to it...You are now sinking with a sinking ship occupied by other unbelieving believers!

God believes in you; loves you and you are special to Him; but are you willing to get out of the boat filled with **unbelieving believers**? Peter is not only remembered as the disciple who began to drown, he is also remembered for being the one who walked on water. Do you want to be remembered for being a doubting Thomas or a true believer? The choice is yours, and no matter what choice you make, God really believes in you! Your success is NOT negotiable. The Winning Image begins as you are reciprocating your belief by believing God. No matter what – you have decided to follow Jesus. So, beginning today, *"Let the words of your mouth and the meditation of your heart be acceptable in His sight."* Believe that you can do all things through Christ that gives you strength...Then believe and have Faith in God. He most assuredly has Faith in You.

And it is so. Manifest!

Let Us Pray:

Heavenly Father forgive me in the Name of Jesus. Forgive me for causing any grief to you Holy Spirit through doubt and unbelief. I receive Your forgiveness and I ask that You help me overcome unbelief. Help me to believe Your Word above any other source in the world—above what my body tells me, above what the doctors tell me, above what friends or family tell me, above what the internet tells me, above what well-meaning Christians tell me. Help me to refuse fear when fear is trying so hard to come upon me. Help me to know and fully accept and receive the love You have for me, because You are LOVE. Help me to honor Your commandment to believe in the Name of Jesus and to love others as He gave commandment. Help me to understand the power and authority You have shared with me freely to overcome any temptation to walk in defeat when I am more than a conqueror. Help me to believe that I can do all things through Christ that gives me strength. Help me to stand firm in knowing that as You are so am I in this world NOW. Help me to identify and rid myself of every soul tie that has incarcerated, blinded or has negatively influenced my soul and therefore my life choices. I want to believe, and I receive the grace to do so. I believe who the Son sets free is free indeed, and I am committed to walk in my newfound freedom. Thank You for Your help Holy Spirit. In Jesus' Mighty Name I declare it to be so.

And it is so! Manifest! Amen.

Soul Session Scripture: *"I do believe: Lord, help my unbelief"* Mark 9:24(b)

Soul Session Song: "I Believe" by Sounds of Blackness

Soul Session #3: COMMAND YOUR SOUL!
(Spirit of Discouragement)

Sometimes, you hear a prophetic word, and you know it is from God. It resonates deep within your spirit, and you know, that you know, it is truth. It may trigger an understanding, or it may steer you towards an action that needs to be taken. It may be designed to heal you at the place you feel most broken. If allowed, it will even shine light in the dark and hidden places of your mind to heal and liberate you from whatever is tied to the seat of your emotions ~ the soul!

One Sunday, I stayed up late as I often do, and began to ponder on how things were going in my life. It was a fact that things were not as I desired, even though the truth was that I was exactly where God desired. This seemingly "wilderness" experience began to overwhelm me… "How long? Too Long!" I heard myself say to myself (negative self-talk is not overrated)! If I was to listen to my voice and concede to my feelings and emotions, I would admit that I was oppressed and even somewhat upset about still being in a "wilderness" situation, with nobody to blame but myself. So besides being oppressed, I was also wallowing in self-pity.

After a period of time passed, I decided to try to shift what was going on in my mind and emotions (soul) and began to play and listen to praise and worship music. Although the Spirit of Heaviness began to lift, the negative seeds that were planted had already taken root, which made it difficult to uproot. Accompanying the Spirit of Heaviness was its twin sister called the Spirit of Escapism. In times past, she has always been the one that would lure me into a desire to escape the hurt, pain, shame, guilt and condemnation of the past through unhealthy choices, followed up with over-the-counter remedies or sleep-aids. When I decided to NOT yield to that temptation, the struggle became more aggressive and the negative thoughts began to overwhelm me. But, like a flood, the LORD came to my rescue and began to lift up a standard. All of a sudden, I heard, "Rhonda, Command Your Soul!"

I knew at that time it was a "Physician Heal Yourself" moment. I also knew God was sending His word to heal me. I sat up and responded by saying:

"Bless the Lord, Oh my soul, and all that is within me, bless his holy name," (Psalm 103:1). I went on to say, "I Command my Soul to Bless the Lord, all that is within me, I command you to bless the Lord. Bless His Holy name. His name is higher than oppression, depression, hurt, guilt or shame. Why, my soul, are you downcast? Why so disturbed within me? **Put your hope in God,** for I will yet praise him, my Savior and my God" (Psalms 42:11). Then I stood up and began to prophesy (edify, exhort and comfort) to myself, as I said, "I Command my Soul, to Bless the Lord!"

And boom! I knew that it was an anointed word! A word meant for me, that I had to receive. Not just in my head or in my spirit, but in my soul (my mind, will, emotions, thoughts, feelings, etc.). It became a rhema word, just for me (Rhema: the voice of the Holy Spirit speaking DIRECTLY TO YOU at the present moment)! After that, my soul began to LEAP! I began to give God a **"YET"** praise. Those words,

"Rhonda, Command Your Soul," changed my mourning into gladness. It did something for me and to me and in me... Joy flooded my soul, and peace began to guard my thoughts and my mind.

Maybe you're in a situation that is causing you hurt, pain, worry, fret, shame, guilt, anxiety or stress. Maybe you're being tempted to go back to something familiar just to ease the thought of the "what if" in your mind. Maybe you are drawn to try to "sleep-through-it-all," or to take over-the-counter medications to get rid of the self-inflicted pain. Maybe your home has all of a sudden become a battlefield, and the voices around you are louder than the still small voice that is trying to get you to hold your peace. Maybe the misunderstandings on your job, or the disagreements with friends have escalated, to the point where you are tired of defending yourself, and you just don't care to reconcile to nothing and no one. Maybe the person, place or thing that you are drawn to (we are drawn away by our own lust), seems more appealing, than doing what is right.

Maybe what you have committed and vowed to do, doesn't seem to even matter anymore. Or maybe, you may have had the thought of not even desiring to live. Your mind and thoughts are coming up with plausible and reasonable excuses to draw from a pool of excuses and reasons. Your emotional triggers are heightened because the flesh is either tired, weary or does not want to submit or die; and every trick in the book is trying to overtake your resolve to live and to go through until you breakthrough the barriers clouding your mind (soul). If any of the above scenarios have hit a nerve, then yes; negative emotions and thoughts have dominated your will and have influenced your mind, thoughts and emotions. You need to Command Your Soul.

Today, we are going to stop. Pause. Think about the goodness of God and A-L-L He's done for you, and then – COMMAND YOUR SOUL! Command your soul to cry out Lord, "I yield, Daddy-God, to you..." Say, "Not my will, but your will be done!"

You may not be feeling it. But it is not about feeling. Faith comes by hearing, so begin to make this declaration out loud. I COMMAND MY SOUL TO BLESS THE LORD!

You may be feeling alone. Or you may feel as though you have been abandoned and rejected, and are asking, "*Where is the God of Elijah? Why is this happening? I've done all You've asked me to do, Lord! When is enough, enough?*" Can I tell you in spite of all you may have done, it will never measure up to what Jesus has already done...Just for YOU! In spite of how you feel, it's **FEAR** – **F**alse **E**vidence **A**ppearing **R**eal.... You ought to have a "not my will, but yours" in your belly on today; and a nevertheless on your tongue....

Declare over yourself:
"*I may feel like giving up, but nevertheless...*"
"*I may have a migraine from this overwhelming pressure, but nevertheless!*"
"*I may have lost my job, but nevertheless.*"
"*I may feel weak or sick in my body, but nevertheless.*"

"I may have been rejected, guilt-ridden or betrayed, but nevertheless."

"My emotions are all over the place, but nevertheless."

"I can't see my way out of this mess, but nevertheless."

"I don't feel loved, wanted, needed or useful, but nevertheless."

"Yes, I'm aggravated, and I'm frustrated with how I've handled things, but nevertheless..."

BUT, Never-The-Less!!!

Many are the afflictions of the righteous, but the Lord God brings them out of them all! (Psalm 34:19) So, **NEVER-THE-LESS**!

Look at Jesus as our example. When He could've come down off of the cross; He did not come down to save Himself, but He decided to die just to save you and me. With His flesh ripped open and nails in His hands and feet, pierced in His side to fulfill prophecy and a crown of thorns on His head, He could've commanded angels to come and rescue Him, but instead, with genuine love for us, He said,

"Father, forgive them, for they know not what they do." Then He went to hell on purpose to set captivity captive! He took back all that belonged to the Father and set them free; and because He did not get down off the cross, even with the weight of all our sin upon His flesh. He remained faithful to His mission as He was crucified and He rose with all power over His flesh and said, *"Now all power is in my hands!"* That's the kind of God we serve. He is a Mighty God! And He did that just so you can walk in freedom now and no matter what you may feel like... *Command Your Soul to "Give Thanks In All Things. For this is the Will of the Father for You" (I Thessalonians 5:18).*

Can I tell you that you need to tell yourself (inner voice) that you must allow your flesh to die too! Nail everything back to the cross that is not like God and just die! Give the flesh no more room to hinder your SOUL from believing and then receiving the goodness of God. The devil is a liar. He is a master deceiver. He has a glimpse of what God wants to do in you, to you and for you; and he can't stop it. But if he gets you to agree with him, (if any touch and agree on anything on earth, you will have what you say), you will sabotage yourself and stop it from manifesting. Remember, as a man thinks, so will that man be!

If the devil can get you so focused on you and not on Jesus, the Author and Finisher of your faith; he will continue to cause your soul to feel like a castaway, causing you to deviate from the original plan and purpose for your life. When you give satan (the enemy) legal access to you, his **"SOUL"** purpose is to abort your purpose, causing you to feel dysfunctional. But Holy Spirit is here, a very present help; to give you the unction to function in what appears to be dysfunction! If you quit, cheat, give up or deviate from God's plan or purpose, because of how you FEEL; what you are saying to JESUS is, *"You did not do enough, and you are not enough."* When in fact, He is MORE than enough! Your flesh is crying out because it does not want to die, it wants to live! The more you allow the dictates of the flesh to dominate; your SOUL is relenting to its carnal and worldly influences. Your soul is now like a pressure-cooker waiting to blow. Before you do, STOP. NOW would be a good time to say, "I COMMAND MY SOUL!"

Command your flesh to come subject to, or divinely align with your soul (mind, will, emotions) -- and as your soul becomes subject and divinely aligned with your human spirit (which houses the Holy Spirit; who is always divinely aligned with Jesus). The Holy Spirit – is He who leads you to the Father. He is waiting with open arms to calm the storm within and to pull you up out of the waters of despair.

Remember, you have been bought with a price. That is, the precious blood of Jesus. And by His stripes you were healed; Spirit, Soul and Body. God is concerned about ALL of YOU and everything that concerns you.

WWJD (What Would Jesus Do), when facing this temptation? He would punish the flesh, and even if His soul was agonizing, He still would say NEVER-THE-LESS. God in heaven breathed into you the breath of life, and you became a LIVING SOUL. When you asked Jesus to come live in you, you became dead to you and alive to Christ, just for such a time as this. Now, command your soul, and bring your soul under the direct influence and supervision of Christ, the anointed one. Not allowing any other distractions, focus on Him who is worthy of your praise, and begin to command your soul…Out of your own mouth say, "*Bless the Lord O my soul and all that is within me.* **I command my soul right now to BLESS THE LORD!**" Come on for about 60 seconds…. COMMAND YOUR SOUL… to Bless the Lord!

My Declarative Prayer for YOU!

"The Spirit of the Lord is upon me, because He has anointed me to bring good news to you, the poor in spirit, and COMMAND YOUR SOUL, (your mind, your will, your emotions, your memory faculty, your paradigm, your intellect, your beliefs, your feelings, your conscious and your subconscious thoughts), to come subject to the Spirit of the Living God.

He has sent me to proclaim release to those who are in captivity. Those who fell captive to their flesh, captive to their thoughts, captive to their lifestyle, to their poor relationships, poor choices, poor decisions, poor health, poor eating habits, to any kind of addictions, destructive escape methods; to those who fell captive to their job, their zip code, even their religious spirit and false responsibility. Any captivity of any kind.

God has anointed me through this writing today to touch your soul and proclaim liberty! He has anointed me to the recovery of sight to the blind; those in the dark - no clue to the truth; those who are in error; have ungodly beliefs, false perceptions and conceptions; wearing colored lenses; anyone who is oppressed, depressed, suicidal thoughts or images, you are commanded to break free. Right now, your soul has been reconciled, restored and favored with God, as I proclaim this the year of the Lord's release and favor," your Kairos moment of Jubilee! .... *And Who the Son sets free is free indeed!* (John 8:36)

And it is so! Manifest!

Say out loud, **I COMMAND MY SOUL!**

Soul Session Scripture: *"The Spirit of the LORD is on me, because he has anointed me to proclaim good news to the poor. He has sent me to proclaim freedom for the prisoners* *and recovery of sight for the blind, to set the oppressed free, to proclaim the year of the LORD's favor."* Luke 4:18-19

Soul Session Song: "I Command My Soul" By Bishop Neil Ellis

Soul Session #4: Dishonesty is NOT the best Policy!

No matter where you are or what you're going through, somebody somewhere is going through it too. The thought that you are the only one dealing with a seemingly unbearable or embarrassing situation is an ungodly belief. *"Beloved, do not be surprised at the fiery trial when it comes upon you to test you, as though something strange were happening to you. But rejoice insofar as you share Christ's sufferings, that you may also rejoice and be glad when his glory is revealed."* 1 Peter 4:12-13

It amazes me that when we are faced with a fiery trial or a hard situation, we have a tendency to desire to put a nice silk dress or a cashmere sweater or if male, a good-looking suit, instead of being honest and transparent. This is the moment where we need to be as the "Emperor in his new clothes" (naked and unashamed). But instead, we model George Benson's classic song titled, *"Masquerade."* This I find very prevalent, each Sunday service, when most attendees are wearing a mask of dishonesty to cover and conceal the truth.

Honesty should be our calling card. Honesty or truth is one of the pieces of God's armor that we should dress in every day. Honesty is the place where we meet with commonalities, form alliances, compare life's notes, prophesy to one another (edify, exhort and comfort), and decide to confess our faults to one another; so, we can be healed. As we travel together on this journey – taking the mask off and revealing the blackheads, blemishes, bruises and even the black eyes – should be welcomed. It should be welcomed because we know that this too shall fade with time and with the right astringent or ice pack (answers or solutions) from the Word of God.

Why are we taught to "fake it until we make it," instead of being strengthened to "FAITH it because we ALREADY made it?" I don't know. The bible says, *"For we walk by faith and not by sight"* (II Corinthians 5:7). For many, we are sight walkers instead. Our senses are in control as we submit to what we see, hear, touch, feel or even taste.

Why do we choose to cover our transgressions and our sin? Why is our reputation more important than our soul's condition? Why do we boost our image with false editing just to fit in? Why are we even encouraged to keep our sin quiet for the sake of others? Why do we put on colored lenses and condone dishonesty? WHY?

I know from personal experience, eventually what is kept in the dark, embellished or restated for popular approval, will come to the light. Once exposed by force, it sometimes will cause irreparable damage to your relationships. Believe me when I say, **Dishonesty is NOT the best Policy!**

The thing that breaks up unity among the family, friends, business partners, fraternity or sorority members, clubs, organizations, mentorships and even churches, is dishonesty. Dishonesty isolates people because only one person can fit behind one mask at a time. Even people with masks try to find connections. Sometimes they forget they're wearing a mask until they are confronted with or need something real. Most are afraid to take off the mask because they feel they'll lose their "friends," "position" or "power," although utterly feeling powerless. They feel trapped by the fact that they'll have to suffer loss to gain what they're really after, which is the freedom to be and live integrally and honestly.

Have you ever reached that place where honesty hurts, because you've been let down, or because you've let people down too many times? We don't need help being realistic or fake. We've worn both those masks before, and we wear them well. The pressure is always on to fabricate our life's circumstance and situation to fit in or to be liked or loved. We become great pretenders, and the stress is real, just to be real! Your soul aches for a breakthrough, but shame or the guilt of dishonesty steals the sliver of happiness that you once felt with friends and those you love. You watch silently from within as your relationships deteriorate, because being honest appears to cost you more than being dishonest. But, can I tell you God knows how to find you and He knows when to speak, what to do and who to use. His love for you will NOT allow you to remain in a dishonest state for long. So, if you've been dishonest for a minute – this is God's way of using me to reach you. He is confronting your dishonest lifestyle even now. God has need of you…. The REAL YOU!

I remember thinking one day, "Will the real Rhonda stand up?" Then I read this scripture which became a source of comfort when I felt the need to lie or "cover up" my sin with a plausible creative explanation (does that sound better?). Just to be clear, you do know that there is no hiding from God or lying to God. He is omniscient and omnipresent. When David sinned, he came to that realization and Psalm 139 became his conclusion to the matter. He wrote:

*"Lord, you have examined me. You know me. You know when I sit down and when I stand up. Even from far away, you comprehend my plans. You study my traveling and resting. You are thoroughly familiar with all my ways. **There isn't a word on my tongue**, Lord that you don't already know completely. You surround me—front and back. You put your hand on me. That kind of knowledge is too much for me; it's so high above me that I can't fathom it. **Where could I go to get away from your spirit?** Where could I go to escape your presence? If I went up to heaven, you would be there. If I went down to hell or the grave, you would be there too! If I could fly on the wings of dawn, stopping to rest only on the far side of the ocean— even there your strong hand would hold me tight! If I said, 'The darkness will*

definitely hide me; the light will become night around me,' even then the darkness isn't too dark for you! Nighttime would shine bright as day, because darkness is the same as light to you! You are the one who created my innermost parts; you knit me together while I was still in my mother's womb. I give thanks to you that I was marvelously set apart. Your works are wonderful—I know that very well. My bones weren't hidden from you when I was being put together in a secret place, when I was being **woven** together in the deep parts of the earth. Your eyes saw my embryo, and on your scroll every day was written that was being formed for me, before any one of them had yet happened. God, your plans are incomprehensible to me! Their total number is countless! If I tried to count them—they outnumber grains of sand! If I came to the very end—I'd still be with you.

Examine me, God! Look at my heart! Put me to the test! Know my anxious thoughts! Look to see if there is any idolatrous way in me, and then lead me on the eternal path!"

Dishonesty clouds your judgment. It clouds your ability to acknowledge your sole purpose on earth. Your purpose in this life is to be "one" with the Father. Dishonesty will not allow that. Your oneness with God is the ONLY way the world knows that He sent Jesus, so the truth can now live inside of you and be on display. As you are one with the Father, then you are empowered to be "one" with each other, learning how to worship Him in spirit and in truth to display His glory.

This is the way the whole world knows that He loves them (John 17:20-23), when they see truth and His love operate in you. *"By **this** everyone will know that you are my disciples, if you love one another."* What is "this?" It is you, imitating His nature, His character, His lifestyle. A dishonest lifestyle does NOT reflect the lifestyle of one who says he is a follower of Christ. It is no coincidence that Jesus said, *"They are not of the world, just as I am not of the world. Sanctify them by the truth; Your word is truth. As You sent Me into the world, I have also sent them into the world"* (John 17:17). HOW? Sanctified in Honesty and Love!

Dishonesty distorts how others see Christ and view the Father. He may be a Good Father but how will the world know that if you are not perceived as a good son or daughter? Remember, it's not by works, so any man can boast. But your WORKS are sometimes ALL others will see. To overcome this conundrum, you must endeavor daily to work out your soul's salvation with fear and trembling, as you endeavor to strive truthfully with the Father, walking in agreement and harmony with His Law (word) and His Love!

Intimacy with the Father is also distorted when we walk in dishonesty. Everything you go through, every prayer you pray — is for the purpose of bringing you further into intimacy with Him. Your relationship with Him is the kind of 'want' that wants more. You go after Him and He goes after you. It's the constant tug of trying to get to each other. It's passionate, it's deeper than deep. However, many never experience this because they refuse to take off their mask. David wrote in Psalm 139, *there is nothing that He does not already know about you and yet, He still loves you so.*

Unfortunately, dishonesty will block true intimacy with your heavenly Father. Any action you take should be in response to Love. The same sacrificial love that was displayed through obedience to the Father's will, *"Not my will, but your will be done"* (Luke 22:42). Instead, we, like Adam and Eve, try to hide behind the fig leaves (cover-ups/lies) of life. Too many of these type decisions and actions of dishonesty move us further and further from the benefits of this intimacy. It's like telling someone you love them, but you're not "in love," therefore you choose not to honor them with honesty. You love them with a mask on. It's all a masquerade!

God does not want you to operate with a sin-consciousness, but at the same time you must realize that we must renounce the hidden things of dishonesty. *"We reject all dishonest, shameful deeds and underhanded methods. We don't try to trick anyone or distort the word of God. We tell the truth before God, and all who are honest know this"* (2 Corinthians 4:2).

He doesn't want you spending too much time working at it; He simply wants you to receive His love and know there's nothing you can do or will do, that will prevent His love from finding you.

It's a popular trend for those who are gifted or skilled to try to use their gifts, talent and skills to work to demonstrate their love for and to the Father. It's a dishonest way of saying love me for what I do and not how I live. This performance-based perception of love gives us a sense of false purpose; we will work hard at looking good instead of being good. We will devote countless of hours helping others, volunteering, working on events, programs, boards and committees, spending our time and energy focusing on everything and everyone, except developing the courage in Christ to walk in truth. This type of displaced love also causes us to walk in dishonesty or ungodly beliefs. We believe that God only loves us because of what we do. No, He loves you because of who you are. He loves your blemishes, blackheads, bruises, black eyes and all. Like a loving Father, He is waiting for you to remove the mask and receive His love to heal, deliver and set you free from the hidden sins of dishonesty. Until you yield to His love (which covers a multitude of sin), don't be surprised when the heat is turned up (so to speak) to get your love and attention drawn back to the desire to be one with Him, rather than alright with everyone else...but not within yourself.

God is not cruel. God doesn't let you hurt just to see how much you can take. The pressure tactics demonically induced and used by life's circumstances and people is allowed only to reveal your insufficiency, so you're forced to come out from behind your mask. Whether you are dealing with historical dishonesty, relational dishonesty, emotional dishonesty, current or future dishonesty, financial dishonesty and so on... there is a love so strong inside of you and for you that is able to do "exceedingly, abundantly, above all you can ever ask or think." Nothing is impossible for our God. TRUST is key. You must trust him enough to replace fear with trust in your God-given ability and power to be free from the lie and to walk in truth. No matter what!

Telling lies and being deceitful is a plague many non-Christian and Christian people suffer alike. Call it a white lie or a dark lie, a lie is still a lie and it is one of the detestable sins before God (Proverbs 6:16-19). It wearies the soul; hurts those we love and slowly eats at our flesh. Once lies and deceit have their claws sunk into the human mind, it is difficult for the tongue to regain its freedom.

Nobody who tells lies will enter heaven (Revelation 21:8, Revelation 21:27, 1 Corinthians 6:9-11), unless you ask for forgiveness and you repent of telling lies. Sin hurts us and separates us from God. When we sin, we die a slow death physically and spiritually. You may be suffering from this plague of telling lies and being deceitful even now. But you can ask God for the forgiveness of your sin, repent of this detestable sin, turn away from lying and deception as God is faithful to forgive you and cleanse you from all unrighteousness.

Today, if your dishonesty is keeping you from knowing His love and receiving his forgiveness, you must believe that He loves you and He has time to wait... Do you?? We don't know how much time we have to wait. While you may choose to wait because you think you have time, life can get pretty lonely. Sooner or later a life of dishonesty will destroy relationships with those who mean the most. A life of dishonesty will not only devour and destroy you, but more importantly, it's goal is to separate you from your most important relationship... with God.

Although God can and will reconcile all things unto himself, why ruin something that you can save today, simply by being honest with Him, yourself and then others? Ask God to give you the courage to change the things you can, beginning today. Something you need to remember... your life is not your own. You can hold onto your image, your plans, and your dishonesty so tightly, that it now has you incarcerated and separated from your one true love! Choose today to be free. Tell the truth and shame the devil. Dishonesty is NOT the Best Policy!

Let Us Pray:

Father forgive me for being deceitful in my words, thoughts and in actions. I know through your word that nobody who is deceitful will dwell in your house or stand in your presence. Deliver me from telling lies, it wearies my soul and puts me in trouble every time with others and especially those I love. Teach me to speak the truth always. Help me to be honest at all times. Keep falsehood and lies far from me. Keep me from deceitful ways; be gracious to me through your law and your love. Keep my tongue from evil and my lips from speaking lies that I may see many good days ahead. Reverse the effects of my deceitful ways. Help me to hate deceits and falsehood but to love your law. Let me establish the truth on my lips and let it endure forever. Give me favor today with those I have wronged in this dishonest state. I thank you for forgiving me as I repent from being dishonest to you and allow Holy Spirit to direct me to others. Go before me and make all crooked paths straight. Allow the spirit of reconciliation with you first and then others to arise. And as I tell the truth and operate in honesty, give me favor with you and with man. This I pray in the name of Jesus.

And it is so. Manifest! Amen!

Soul Session Scripture: *Lie not one to another, seeing that ye have put off the old man with his deeds.* - Colossians 3:9-10

Soul Session Song: "You Know Me" by Steffany Frizzell

Soul Session #5: Forgive and You Will Be Forgiven!

(Spirit of Unforgiveness)

I remember a time that God took me into the deepest realm of forgiveness that I had ever experienced. I was feeling wronged by a Christian Sister. I was offended and felt that I did not deserve the false judgments and things she was saying about me, mainly to other people. She took an incident she heard from another wounded person and because she "heard" something similar about me in the past from someone else, she went to someone I really loved and put a nail in the coffin that was already closing fast, due to other things that were said!! (Whew... could you keep up with all that?!) Hearsay and gossip!! They can hurt both ways every time!

The enemy really wanted to destroy this covenant relationship and he was being very successful in using others. To say I played no role in it would be a lie. But what this sister said, and how it was done...was just wrong! It was a flat-out opinionated lie!

I was angry and hurt. I immediately thought about Proverbs 6:16, *"There are six things the Lord hates, seven are detestable to Him."* And as I sat in the seat of judgment, I felt she qualified for all six things God hates. I even recall making a checklist to take before God:

- A proud look √
- A lying tongue √
- A heart that devises wicked schemes √
- Feet that are quick to rush to evil √
- A false witness who pours out lies √
- A person who stirs up conflict in the community √

Have you ever wanted to go before God and pray a "Davidic" type prayer regarding those who wronged you? You know like...

"Lord may those who try to destroy me be humiliated and put to shame. May those who take delight in my trouble be turned back in disgrace." Psalm 40:14

"Let evil recoil on those who slander me; in your faithfulness destroy them." Psalm 54:5

"And in Your lovingkindness, cut off my enemies and destroy all those who afflict my soul, for I am your servant." Psalm 143:2

Ahhh, the Old Testament...on some days, the good 'ole days, really appeal to me!

But then... God quickly reminded me of how on more than one occasion, I too was found in Proverbs 6:16-19. But it was during those times, these were the prayers of David I would recite:

"Have mercy on me, O God, according to your unfailing love; according to your great compassion blot out my transgressions. Wash away all my iniquity and cleanse me from my sin." Psalm 51:1-2

"For the sake of your name, LORD, forgive my iniquity, though it is great." Psalm 25:11

"I am your servant; deal with me in unfailing love and teach me your decrees. Amen." Psalm 119:124

The bible tells us to, *"bless those who persecute you; bless and do not curse. Rejoice with those who rejoice; mourn with those who mourn. Live in harmony with one another. Do not be proud but be willing to associate with people of low position. Do not be conceited. Do not repay anyone evil for evil. Be careful to do what is right in the eyes of everybody. If it is possible, as far as it depends on you, live at peace with everyone. Do not take revenge, my friends, but leave room for God's wrath, for it is written: 'it is mine to avenge; I will repay,' says the Lord. On the contrary: If your enemy is hungry, feed him; if he is thirsty, give him something to drink. In doing this, you will heap burning coals on his head. Do not be overcome by evil but overcome evil with good"* (Romans 12:14-21). Be merciful, just as your Father is merciful. *"Do not judge and you will not be judged. Do not condemn, and you will not be condemned. **Forgive, and you will be forgiven"** (Luke 6:36-37).

A root of bitterness can grow up in a person because of unforgiveness. This root can be buried deep inside your heart and can block the flow of God's love from penetrating deep within your soul, making it difficult to truly encounter

Him and His love. Unforgiveness is a major cause of depression for many people, but they are not aware of the soul ties that leads to both dangerous spiritual and physical side effects.

One of the causes and effects of the unforgiveness is that it is an inside job that affects us internally but causes us to respond outwardly in dishonesty toward people. Sometimes we do and say things that hurt us very deeply. Sometimes we are hurt by the ones that are closest to us. Sometimes people are hurt in childhood, at the most vulnerable time of life, leaving wounds that we think are healed, but they have left scars that still remind us of the wound; and yes, wounded people wound people.

These painful hurts can be buried so deep within us that we may be unaware that we are still carrying some resentment toward the person who hurt us and transfer these buried emotions toward others. Unforgiveness is simply a form of pride. When we choose unforgiveness over forgiveness, it equates to rejecting God's love and inviting Satan in. *"Be angry, and do not sin: Do not let the sun go down on your wrath, nor give place to the devil"* (Ephesians 4:26-27). *"Make every effort to live in peace with all men and to be holy; without holiness no one will see the Lord. **See to it that no one misses the grace of God and that no bitter root grows up to cause trouble and defile many"** (Hebrews 12:14-15).* If your "root of bitterness" rejects God's grace, it will continue to grow stronger and stronger. In doing so, it will cause trouble for you and for others. Unforgiveness is one of the most destructive spirits known to mankind.

Did you know that **unforgiveness is an unforgivable sin,** which allows Satan an open door into your life? The bible says it like this: *"For if you forgive men when they sin against you, your heavenly Father will also forgive you. **But if you do not forgive men their sins, your Father will not forgive your sins"** (Matthew 6:14-15).

Jesus said, *"But I tell you: Love your enemies and pray for those who persecute you, that you may be sons of your Father in heaven. He causes his sun to rise on the evil and the good and sends rain on the righteous and the unrighteous. If you love those who love you, what reward* *will you get? Are not even the tax collectors doing that? And if you greet only your brothers, what are you doing more than others? Do not even pagans do that? Be perfect, therefore, as your heavenly Father is perfec*t" (Matthew 5:44-48).

I always thought that I was good at forgiveness, and I believe people that know me would agree with the thought, that because of some awful situations I have gone through in my life, I did real good let go of the hostility and forgive. I've turned cheeks all too often. I've taken the blame for the sake of the gospel and the relationship. I've gone out of my way to be the bigger person, even though it made me feel so small. However, this time, the Lord took me to a new dimension of forgiveness that I had never known before. I soon realized that what I thought was forgiveness actually was not. Until you are able with all sincerity to go before the throne of grace in front of the mercy seat and plead for God to forgive the people who have wronged or offended you... you have not fully forgiven.

Just as Jesus hanging in agony on the cross, looked down at the people killing Him and said, *"Father forgive them, for they do not know what they are doing" (Luke 23:34).* God wants us to come to that point in our life. We all need to get to the point where you are dead to yourself and have surrendered all of your rights be angry, hurt, offended, embarrassed, ready to punish, and to judge the other person, you are not ready to truly forgive and therefore; you will forfeit the most humbling Christ-like spiritual experience you can ever have. Although very painful to give up all your rights and die to yourself, God gives more grace to the humble. The Bible says, *"God resists the proud; But gives grace to the humble"* (James 4:6).

Once I submitted to Holy Spirit's truth and not my feelings, I felt that burden lift. I felt the most awesome presence of God come upon me. *"Blessed are the merciful (compassionate), for they shall obtain mercy (compassion)"* (Matthew 5:7). I felt God's compassion overwhelm me and fill me to the overflowing state. He filled me and the anger, pain, hurt left.

We have to be very careful to not let ourselves become offended at other people, because we will be judged the same way we judge others. *"Judge not, that you be not judged. For with what judgment you judge, you will be judged; and with the measure you use, it will be measured back to you. It's better to have mercy than judgment"* (Matthew 7:1-2).

We must forgive everyone that offends us, and everyone that sins against us. *"For if you forgive men when they sin against you, your heavenly Father will also forgive you. But if you do not forgive men their sins, your Father will not forgive your sins"* (Matthew 6:14-15).

Forgiveness is an action of compassion and an act of love. *"But love your enemies, do good, and lend, hoping for nothing in return; and your reward will be great, and you will be sons of the Most High. For He is kind to the unthankful and evil. Therefore, be merciful, just as your Father also is merciful. Judge not, and you shall not be judged. Condemn not, and you shall not be condemned. Forgive, and you will be forgiven. Give, and it will be given to you: good measure, pressed down, shaken together, and running over will be put into your bosom. For with the same measure that you use, it will be measured back to you"* (Luke 6:35-38).

Note: Not the money scripture you thought it was, is it?

"Let us then approach the throne of grace with confidence, so that we may receive mercy and find grace to help us in our time of need" (Hebrews 4:16).

"Every high priest is selected from among men and is appointed to represent them in matters related to God, to offer gifts and sacrifices for sins. He is able to deal gently with those who are ignorant and are going astray, since he himself is subject to weakness. This is why he has to offer sacrifices for his own sins, as well as for the sins of the people" (Hebrews 5:1-3).

The bible instructs us to go and be reconciled to our brother/sister before we even bring a gift to the Lord.

After my true encounter with God, I wanted to reconcile, but it seemed impossible because we were unable, and she seemed unwilling to even communicate so that we could reconcile. One night when this was a heavy weight upon my soul, I began crying out to the Lord not even knowing what to say or pray. I sometimes just groaned in my Spirit, even groaning out loud at times. For about two hours I sought the Lord and His help. I truly had a burden for her soul and the heaviness that was in mine concerning it.

At one point, it finally occurred to me that the Lord must be trying to teach me something because it seems always at my lowest points of despair; God gives me the greatest revelations. Even as a young preacher, Dr. McKenzie (Pastor & Spiritual Father) would always ask me to preach when I was at the lowest point of my life. He shared, that it is in that place Holy Spirit can do what He does through me unhindered. Less of Me ~ More of Him. So, I asked, "Lord, what are you trying to teach me?" Within a few minutes the revelation began. I felt that I should pray what I had been teaching others to pray; and that was for God to have grace, mercy, and compassion upon the person who I felt had wronged me. Immediately, I thought, "no, maybe God is saying He needs to deal with this person and 'teach her a lesson' as well." Recognizing that this judgmental spirit was still alive and well on my part, and that I had a very wrong attitude, I again asked God to forgive me. I stayed in that posture until I truly desired to ask God to grant me repentance. God knows if you are real or not. He knows if you are really ready to change or just pretend to do so. Listen…You can't hurry God nor can you fool him!

Then one night I was broken, and I cried out, "God please, create in me a clean heart and a right spirit within." Then I proceeded to pray for her that God would have grace, mercy and compassion on her, everything that concerns her and any others that may be involved.

I always knew it was the right thing to do since, "Obedience is better than sacrifice" (I Samuel 15:22). It wasn't the first time or the second time I prayed; but the same day just like Job, as soon as I forgave and began praying for her, I felt in myself began to shift and literally and spiritually move into the presence of God. That's when the anger faded and the burden I was falsely bearing started to lift. I then proceeded to thank God for forgiveness; as all I desired to do was repent for my wrong. I repented for even the appearance of evil or wrongdoing. I confessed my wrong, even though He already knew it. Then God showed me my wrong in a situation with my sister too. What? I thought I forgave her in prayer. My sister and others I felt wronged me. Not that I was perfect, but yet again, I started to name off each person and each offense I felt was done against me? Each time I named an offense, God showed me my wrong time and time again. I felt the heavy burdens lift from my soul over and over AGAIN, once I repented. When I named the last sin of unforgiveness that I could think of, my soul finally felt free.

What was so scary about the situation was that I still functioned in my gift and in my calling. It is a dangerous thing to be functioning in your gift and calling while in sin. The bible says, "*Not everyone who says to Me, 'Lord, Lord' will enter the kingdom of heaven, **but only he who does the will of My Father in heaven.** Many will say to Me on that day, 'Lord, Lord did we not prophesy in Your name, and in*

Your name drive our demons and perform many miracles?'
Then I will tell them plainly, 'I never knew you; depart from
Me, you workers of iniquity (lawlessness!)'." You see, you
can fool some of the people some of the time, but you will
never fool God.

So, what is the will of the Father? **To Love HIM more than
you love yourself. Forgive and to be forgiven. To repent,
for the kingdom of God is at hand!**

Immediately I felt that once my heart changed, the situation
changed. Holy Spirit reminded me of the words of Jesus, *"If
you forgive the sins of any, they are forgiven them; if you
retain the sins of any, they are retained."* So, since I forgave,
I knew that the young lady and my sisters' sins were fully
forgiven too.

Now manifestly, at that time, we did not yet physically
reconcile, but it is not because I did not try. Even though I
wanted to say, "Lord, well at least I tried, but she keeps
rejecting me," God would not let me get an 'E' for Effort.
The process would NOT be complete until we were totally

reconciled. So, I continued to pursue her for my total deliverance to be established. I continued to pray for my sister, believing that soon she would be set free from the enemy's deception as well, and we would be reconciled.

"Above all, love each other deeply, because love covers over a multitude of sins" (1 Peter 4:8 NIV).

It was almost a year later, when I was contacted by someone needing help with a project. I suggested a few people that I knew were more than qualified for the task, and shared that I would personally vet them for the project before recommending them. Later on, that day, Holy Spirit began to speak to me about recommending her for the job. Instantaneously, I knew it was not only the right thing to do, but I knew she would be the right fit for the project. I did not call her to vet her; I simply called the person back and highly recommended her for the job.

It was at the Reveal and Release Party of a mentee, that God revealed and released some things as well. The host called me over to where they were standing and said, "Rhonda, I just want to thank you again for recommending her. She was perfect for the project. Your glowing recommendation sold us, and we could not have been happier with the results of your final choice." It was at that moment I saw God's humility cloak her as she finally gave me eye contact and said, "You recommended me for this job?" Before I could say a word, the host said, "Oh, you didn't know? I thought she called you before she called us. Yes, if it had not been for her, there would be no this!!" Wow, talking about a Reveal and Release party! This opened the door to several conversations that eventually led to healing what was fractured.

We were never best friends, so I did not expect a fairy-tale ending to the story, but in my obedience, it also led to the coffin re-opening of a covenant relationship that I thought was lost.

I was attending a conference and I heard God say, *"I am mending what was broken."* At the time I did not know what God was speaking of, but on the second day of the conference, someone came to me and said that I was requested to step outside. I've learned that when you hurt someone, you can never dictate how they heal, but you must allow God to reveal what He wants to heal. As you remain constant in prayer and demonstrate the love of Christ at all costs, reconciliation is inevitable. Even if someone vows to never forgive you in their heart. God is constantly at work if you walk in forgiveness and love. Remember, *"Greater love has no man than to lay down his life for a friend"* (John 15:13).

What most don't realize (well maybe a few); I probably hurt more than she did. I hurt more because this was an important relationship to me. I knew my wrong fractured our relationship and because I could not repair it, I spent many years punishing myself. So not only was God waiting for her to forgive me, but I truly believe I held up that process since I had to first forgive myself. Once I forgave myself, God finally opened her heart to forgive me as well. It did not happen overnight. This was almost two years later when this meeting would finally take place, and what once was broken was reconciled. There have been many other God has allowed my offense to be forgiven and when I forgave, other important relationships in my life begin to reconcile and heal too.

So, how do you know if you have truly forgiven someone that has hurt you?

Do you say or think things like this? "I forgive the person, but I will let God deal with them."

Do you say things like: "I forgive the person, but I do not want to see them, hear them or talk to them again." How would you feel if God said to you, "I forgive you, but I've decided to ignore you and not speak to you." Would you feel forgiven? That is not forgiveness. **God's forgiveness always restores.**

Do you still feel bitter, get upset or have any anger or bad feelings toward the person? When you fully forgive the person, anger will be replaced with empathy for them and then ultimately, redemption and LOVE!

Do you still hold on to the memory of the wrong done to you, thinking about it often? True forgiveness forgets the hurt and pain, if not always the situation. The healing process of forgiveness causes the memory of the pain to disappear, as if it did not happen. When God forgives, He also forgets it forever, as if it never occurred (The Sea of Forgiveness).

Do you have trouble being merciful toward others even after they ask for forgiveness? If so, when you don't have mercy, it is hard for you to believe that God has mercy and compassion for you. Forgiving others makes it easier to be able to forgive yourself and accept God's forgiveness in your life. *"Blessed are the merciful, for they shall obtain mercy"* (Matthew 5:7).

The word **blessed** means to be happy, joyful, merciful, grateful, oppression and depression-free. Sometimes we may think that we really and truly have forgiven the person, but in reality, we really have not. Our surrender and obedience to forgive is so powerful. When we forgive, then God forgives them too. "Again, Jesus said, *'Peace be with* *you! As the Father has sent me, I am sending you.' And with that he breathed on them and said, 'Receive the Holy Spirit. If you forgive anyone his sins, they are forgiven; if you do not forgive them, they are not forgiven.' When you fully forgive, God's peace will rest upon you, and the Holy Spirit will comfort you,"* (John 20:21-23 NIV).

This is how to enter into the healing, forgiveness, compassion, mercy, and grace, which is an extension of His Love. Pray to the Father. Posture yourself in humility. Get on your knees. Get into a quiet place. Enter into a prayer closet or designated room. Wherever you find your space, dedicate that place as your place to cry out to God. After you pray for yourself, begin to pray for the person that has hurt you. Approach the throne of grace, in front of the mercy seat, and petition your Father in heaven to please forgive this person. Ask God almighty to pour out His grace, mercy, and compassion upon this person and in this person. Name off every sin that has been done by you against him and others. Allow God to reveal them to you so He can help them and release them from you. It's time to leave them behind. Plead for their souls just as Jesus hanging upon the cross in agony looked down on the people murdering Him and said, *"Father forgive them for they know not what they are doing,"* you pray the same. Remember, Job was healed AFTER he prayed for his friends. Then God blessed him with double for all of his troubles.

Ask God to please forgive each sin done against you individually. As you ponder on those things, will to forgive, that you might live! Allow God to forgive you and release you from the burden of unforgiveness. Name every emotion/hurt you have been falsely carrying. God will begin to lift off and remove each one of them. You will know when they are all gone.

*"Who is wise and understanding among you? Let him show it by his good life, by deeds done in the humility that comes from wisdom. **But if you harbor bitter envy and selfish ambition in your hearts**, do not boast about it or deny the truth. Such "wisdom" does not come down from heaven but is earthly, unspiritual, of the devil. For where you have envy and selfish ambition, there you find disorder and every evil practice. But the wisdom that comes from heaven is first of*

all pure; then peace-loving, considerate, submissive, full of mercy and good fruit, impartial and sincere. Peacemakers who sow in peace raise a harvest of righteousness" (James 3:13-18 NIV).

I have no doubt that many of you are carrying some deep wounds that you've carried for months, maybe even years. When you think about that person who hurt you, it's still as fresh as if it happened this morning. The pain is still there, and you're still filled with resentment. You say, *"Why in the world should I forgive the person who hurt me so much? You have no idea what they did, or how much they hurt me. It's unforgivable! Why should I offer grace to that person?"* What you fail to realize is, until you graciously forgive those who've hurt you, God will not graciously forgive you, for every time you hurt Him, which is an immeasurable number.

You will never have to forgive anyone else more than Jesus Christ has already forgiven you. You should consider that you haven't always received the punishment that you deserved. God has been gracious with you. Now it's your time, your moment, to be gracious with and toward others.

Scientists tell us that resentment is the unhealthiest emotion there is; and the bible tells us that it is as rottenness to the bones (joint pain, bone degeneration, aches, low bone density or arthritis, rheumatoid arthritis anyone?). **These ungodly emotions always hurt you more than they hurt anybody else!** Resentment, anger, bitterness and unforgiveness will not change the past, and they won't solve the problem. It doesn't even make you feel better. In fact, it makes you feel worse.

"Be careful that none of you fails to respond to the grace which God gives, for if he does there can very easily spring up in him a bitter spirit which is not only bad in itself but can also poison the lives of many others" (Hebrews 12:15).

The reason why some of you have a hard time forgiving is because you don't feel forgiven. Now right now. Right where you are, God is going to allow you to let go and let God. For the rest of this week when God brings anyone to your mind, write it down, make note of it. Then take them and that memory into prayer, beginning with forgiveness, then repentance. Accepting the things, you cannot change, but knowing God can. Prayer must precede the process.

Then you must take action steps as directed by Holy Spirit. **What God reveals; He wants to heal**. It's time to set others FREE so you can be FREE! Let's Forgive.

Let Us Pray:

Father, in the Name of Jesus, we affirm our re-dedication to loving you and loving others, to hear your heart and to find ourselves in your word so you can help us remove the barriers that seem to sour our relationships and keep us at a distance. Heal our short tempers, our crabbiness, our rudeness, and our critical spirits. Heal our fear of rejection and the grudges we hold; against one another, against our parents, spouses, our siblings, children, relatives, friends, supervisors, pastors, church, even financial institutions that may have denied us what we thought we needed. Manifestly take away the pain, embarrassment, hurt, guilt and shame and if there is any condemnation, we denounce it now in Jesus name. We too stand guilty of the blame game, victim-mentality, selfishness, pride and arrogance. Many of us have lived beyond our means and we've become angry and irrational and embrace ideologies that protect our stuff and not our relationships. We need your help to stop contributing to the hurt of others, even when we are right. Help us take the wrong for the sake of reconciliation and restoration. We believe in the power of your grace to change our lives, as we promise to once again be open to walk in the sufficiency of your grace.

I make a fresh commitment to You to live in forgiveness, unity, peace and harmony, not only with the other brothers and sisters of the Body of Christ, but also with my friends, associates, neighbors, co-workers, church family and family members, that I feel have hurt me. Father, it appears to be a hard thing to let it go. But nothing is too hard for you. I let go of all malice, anger, bitterness, resentment, envy, strife, and unkindness in any form. I give no place to the devil, in Jesus' Name.

Now Father, I ask for Your forgiveness for me and for (name them). By faith, I receive forgiveness for me and those who have hurt me intentionally and maybe even unknowingly. As I forgive and let go, I thank you that I am cleansed from all unrighteousness through Jesus Christ. I ask You to forgive and release all who have purposefully wronged and hurt me. I choose to forgive and release them from their wrong doings. Do not deal with them in your sore displeasure, but with mercy and loving-kindness. From this moment on, I purpose to walk in love, to seek peace, to live in harmony and in agreement with the Word of God. I shall conduct myself toward others in a manner that is pleasing to You.

Bless each of us with a peaceful spirit and a desire to be reconciled with one another. And as we sleep, deal with us in dreams on tonight, Lord. More importantly, speak to me about me. Reveal what you want to reveal; to heal and not conceal. Create in me a clean heart and renew a right spirit within me. I open up my heart to you and I surrender it all. I will to forgive so that I can live in harmony with you. I choose to forgive, Lord. I choose to forgive, so that I can be forgiven and live life more abundantly, no longer a slave to sin, free from all iniquity. I know that NOW I am in right standing with you and Your ears are attentive to my prayers. It is written in Your Word that the love of God has been poured into my heart by the Holy Spirit who is given to me. I believe that love flows not only into my heart but into the lives of everyone I know, and I forgive, that I may be filled with and abound in the fruits of righteousness which bring glory and honor to You; My Savior and my Lord, in Jesus' Name.

I believe and therefore I speak…. And it so. Manifest! Amen.

Soul Session Scripture: *"Bear with each other and forgive one another if any of you has a grievance against someone. Forgive as the Lord forgave you."*
Colossians 3:13

Soul Session Song: "A Heart that Forgives" by Kevin Levar

Soul Session #6: I Think Myself Happy (Defeating the Spirit of Despair and Oppression)

Scripture tells us in Acts 26:1-2a that King Agrippa said to Paul, *"You have permission to speak for yourself."* So, Paul motioned with his hand and began his defense by saying: *"King Agrippa, I think myself happy..."*

Say that aloud for yourself: **I THINK MYSELF HAPPY!!!**

Put yourself in Paul's shoes for a moment. You've been arrested for doing nothing more than praying in the Jewish Temple. You have been charged with a capital offense of which you are completely innocent, and now you have been unjustly imprisoned for two long years! At last, you have a chance to tell your side of the story, to speak on your behalf. What would your statement in defense be? Would the first words out of your mouth be, *"Your Honor, I think myself happy?"* I suspect you may opt to say something different like:

"I think myself Sad..."

"I think myself Mad!"

"I think myself Mistreated!"

"I think myself a victim of false imprisonment."

"I think myself a victim of false witnesses, liars and cruel intentions."

"I think I want to be FREE..."

But not Paul. Paul's confession wasn't that he was sad, mad, mistreated or a victim of any kind. His confession was, **"I Think Myself Happy!"** He is found standing before King Agrippa and the Governor, Felix facing further imprisonment simply because he chose to "PRAY OPENLY," as a New Testament believer.

Paul now has the opportunity to begin his opening statement by presenting the facts of his case, but instead, His opening statement is – **"I Think Myself Happy!"**

I love that! I want to be like that.

Paul knew a secret that only few people knew. He knew the secret to happiness. Most people think that happiness is what happens to you when good things happen in your life.

The Bible says something else. The Bible teaches that calamity happens to us all. It says, *"Many are the afflictions of the righteous, BUT the Lord God delivers us out of them all"* (Psalm 34:19). It also says, *"IN ALL THINGS give thanks; for this is the will of the FATHER for you in the name of our Lord Jesus Christ"* (1 Thessalonians 5:18).

Happiness comes in knowing that no matter what state you are in, or in what circumstance you find yourself; God is in control. This situation was **ALLOWED** to **BRING GOD GLORY.** What Paul experienced was an opportunity given by God for him to eloquently speak about the 'Love of Christ' and His saving power for ALL who believed. He had the honor of telling of God's grace, love and mercy. This God, the only true and living God is an AWESOME God! Paul also understood that good things come from within from The One who lives within. Therefore, our happiness is our choice. It's not what happens to you that will determine your happiness. It's your answer (reaction) to what happens to you that determines your happiness!

It is said that happiness is a state of mind. It differs greatly from joy. We as believers should understand that joy comes from God and God alone. Joy is the state not predicated upon your circumstance. This world nor any man cannot give you joy, and this world nor man cannot take it away. No matter what bothers you, joy is ever present. Even in the midst of bereavement, when our hearts are yet broken and heavy, we are told, *"weeping may endure for a night, but joy comes in the morning"* (Psalm 30:5). We know that there is a better state of being beyond what our senses convey. We are further told that we don't grieve like the non-believers. Why? Because even though it may be deemed a sad occasion, the scripture says, *"Blessed are they that mourn, for they shall be comforted"* (Matthew 5:4).

Scripture does not say happiness comes in the morning; it says "JOY." The Joy of our Lord gives us strength to persevere in any and through all situations and circumstances. So, with joy, you and I can do as Paul did and think ourselves happy, no matter what! David said, *"I have hidden your word in my heart that I might not sin against you"* (Psalm 119:11). Without the Spirit of God and the

Word of God on the inside, there can be no real joy. God's Spirit moves within His people and His Spirit produces a fruit or an extension of Who He is called, "Joy."

Man cannot mess with God's Joy (in my MC Hammer voice, "Can't Touch This"). Even in the midst of problems --we can still have joy. Even in the midst of folks being ugly toward us – we can still have joy. Even when we are under spiritual attack – we can still have joy. Even when your money is less than your bills – we can still have joy.

The Joy the Lord is not contingent upon your circumstance, your situation or your emotional state; it has been freely given, so you must freely receive it. You must know that no matter what, with joy, you can **Think Yourself Happy!**

Without joy, happiness is simply a state of mind. *"And as a man thinks in his heart or mind, so is he"* (Proverbs 23:7). Many of us are confused when it comes to understanding the difference between joy and happiness. The two words are not interchangeable. We as Christians should properly understand the message that Paul has delivered to us. Paul has given us a secret weapon. Joy reigns on the inside. JOHN 15:11, says *"these things I have spoken to you, that my joy may remain in you, and that your joy may be full."*

Our JOY remains in us.

Our JOY springs Eternal.

Our JOY is full because it is interconnected to the Lord.

The Lord's joy placed in us *"remains"* in us and it is full because it is not based upon what we have or don't have – what we've done or have not done. Joy actually is a person, or for some, the character or nature of a person. That person or the fruit thereof is CHRIST!

Have you ever seen Christians in the Church that seems to never smile? You've ever seen Christians in the community that always seem like they are mad, unsatisfied, always frowning, argumentative, angry and unhappy; yet they are saved, in the Church, support things within the life of the Church, and they give and support the ministry financially?

Still, they never seem to smile!

The problem is not found in their joy. The problem resides in their Happiness. Happiness is rooted in our desires, pleasures and self-beneficial situations. For example:

When there is money in our pockets – we are happy. But when our money is low – we are no longer happy. When it is payday – we are happy. Three days later – we are no longer happy. Riding up and down the highway with a tank full of gas – we are happy. But when the gas tank is empty – we are no longer happy. Buy a new house – we are happy. But when the payment/mortgage is due – we are no longer happy.

To sum it up, joy and happiness come from two different power sources. Happiness finds his root in our soulish realm and anything tied or connected to it can influence our mood or state of being. Therefore, we can be greatly influenced in selfish or worldly desires, things or situations. Whereas joy is rooted in our relationship with the Lord and is influenced by Holy Spirit leading and guiding us to a higher truth. Joy says, no matter what the facts may be or as we are going through any circumstance, our hope, faith and strength is in the one who allowed the situation to occur. Why? So, He can eventually get the glory.... if you let Him.

When your soul has been brought subject or is submitted to your spirit (which is filled with Holy Spirit), then no matter what happens or what state you're in -- you can think yourself happy. You have a power-source within that already defeated despair and oppression.

If we feed our soul with the Word of God and add the daily supplements of the best and good thoughts, we grow stronger and are able to defer to the joy of the Lord while we are thinking about *aligning how we feel with how we truly are.*   While we are continually being exposed to the experiences in the world, we must remember, we are in the world, but not of it. Or at least we are not supposed to be.

When we understand that we can defeat "Unhappiness," then we will be like Paul and be able to say in the midst of any horrific circumstance or surroundings...**I THINK MYSELF HAPPY**!

Daniel in the Lion's Den – I Think Myself Happy

Shadrach, Meshach, Abednego – furnace of fire – I Think Myself Happy

Jeremiah, thrown in a Mud Pit – I Think Myself Happy

Now let's make this personal:

When I am faced with trials and tribulations – I Think Myself Happy

When I am down to my last dime – I Think Myself Happy

When I feel rejected, misused and misunderstood – I Think Myself Happy

(I feel my preach voice coming on! Smile)

When I am pressured, perplexed and don't know what to do – I Think Myself Happy

You may now be asking: *"Well Rhonda, how do I think myself happy when all this is going on around me?"*

No matter what goes on in life, you must think and contend for happiness. God is concerned with everything that concerns you. He invested in your future with His Son's life. Your debts (sin and trespasses) have been paid in FULL. You owe no man nothing but love!! So, even in the midst of the most difficult circumstance, whatever you are faced with, it may be uncomfortable; but joy is ever present. *"The Joy of the Lord is my strength"* (Nehemiah 8:10). That's why Paul could say with confidence, *"when I am weak that's when I'm strong,"* (2 Corinthians 12:10) … and WE can say with him –*"when I am troubled on every side, I am not distressed; I may be perplexed, but not in despair; persecuted, but not forsaken; cast down, but not destroyed"* Why? Because I **Think Myself Happy!**

Let Us Pray:

Lord, sometimes it seems so difficult to be cheerful or happy when I am overwhelmed by the challenges of life. But as I learn how to seek Your face and keep my eyes fixed on You only, I will remember that all things shall work together for my good. God, You said in Your word that if we will seek You, You will transform us and renew our minds, so that we will know Your will concerning us. I humbly submit myself to Your will, Your way and Your Word. Take me and mold me more into Your image and likeness. Lead me away from darkness and despair into Your marvelous light (hope and truth). Guide my steps each, and every day, and bless my life and the life of my loved ones. Father, You promised to never leave us nor forsake us. You are a very present help in the time of need. Lord if there ever was a need, I need You now. At the very moment my thoughts are not Word conscious but world conscious, help me to focus on Your goodness and not on my circumstance. I pray that as I seek You, my emotions will come subject to Your will for my life, as the Peace of God that surpasses all understanding begin to rule and reign even now in my heart and mind in Christ Jesus' mighty Name. Father lift me up where I belong. Let me find myself under the shadow of Your wings, sitting in heavenly places with You Lord Jesus, as everything is now under my feet. No matter what it looks like, feels like, sounds like, old things will pass away, and all things will become new. I put my hope in You Lord and I pray that my thoughts will remain fixed and focused on Your goodness and Your mercies that are new every morning. Great is thy faithfulness. Let me always remember to praise You even more as I thank You in all things. Right now, I think on things that are of a good report as I redirect my attention to the love and safety of You and in believing Your word over every circumstance. Father God, I will continue to pray and praise without ceasing; and as I do, in every situation, Your joy strengthens my once falling heart and emotions and now, **I Think Myself Happy!!**

And it is so. Manifest! Amen!

Soul Session Scripture: *"A cheerful heart is good medicine, but a crushed spirit dries up the bones."* Proverbs 17:22

Soul Session Song: *"You Make Me Happy"* by Tasha Cobbs

Soul Session #7: Rejecting Rejection

(Spirit of Rejection) - 4 Part Series

Part One - Rejecting Rejection - *Performance Oriented and Driven*

At one time or another, many of us experienced some form of rejection, but have not understood its nature or its effects. The rejection you faced may have been something relatively minor—or it may have been so devastating that it affected your whole life and all your relationships.

Here are some common examples: The color of your skin, country or island you were born, nationality, race, community or culture. Maybe, you were not chosen to play on a school sports team or you were chosen last; your first boyfriend or girlfriend broke up with you and began dating someone who you perceived looked better than you. Maybe you did not receive enough votes to get the position; you were not perceived to be your parents favorite child; or you did not get accepted at the college of your choice; you were laid off from your job for an unexplained good reason; the bank denied your home or auto loan. Maybe you lived with the pain that comes because you never felt love from your father or because you sensed your mother didn't want you; or maybe you are the product of a single parent or born out of wedlock or from infidelity and your parent's marriage ended because of IT, but you blame YOU. Maybe it is because your marriage ended in divorce after betrayal of your spouse cheating on you. Maybe you were told you weren't pretty enough, smart enough, fast enough, brave enough, tall enough, fine enough, thin enough, light-skinned enough or could not dance or sing or act or play an instrument or sport as well as a sibling, relative or someone else.

Well, whatever the reason, it may have been a fact to some, but it was not God's truth. Truth lies behind the basis of an appearance. The facts presented do not become your truth until you believe it, or until you touch and agree with it (The Power of Agreement is strong and binding). If your response to any of the above was wrong or not beneficial, if these common examples caused you pain, hurt or offended you; then more than likely you are troubled or challenged with the Spirit of Rejection.

Experiences such as these leave semi-permanent to permanent wounds, whether you are aware of them or not. But I have good news for you! God can heal you from the wounds that come from rejection, help you to accept yourself, and enable you to show His love to yourself and to others in spite of what others may have done, said or even what you have done or said to yourself. But before you can receive His help, you must recognize the nature of your problem. Because what God reveals, He wants to heal!

If rejection was a fruit tree, at first it is just a seed that is planted. But, that seed is soon watered and fertilized and in time, it would bear a lot of fruit which can widely vary from one person to another. Some of the common **symptoms** of rejection include:

- Rebellion in both children and adults.
- Fabricated personalities (being somebody you aren't, in order to be accepted).
- The tendency to reject others, so that you aren't the first one to be rejected.

- A tendency to always wonder if a person rejects or accepts you.

- The need to fit in or be accepted by others and be a part of everything.

- Self-pity where a person feels bad when they may not be a part of the in-crowd. Believing no one wants to be with them, then alienating themselves.

- Inability to be corrected or receive constructive criticism or correction (A person who has a hard time admitting they are wrong, or receiving constructive criticism has an underlying problem with rejection. How do we know that? Because you are basing your identity, who they are, upon your ability to be right about everything).

- Rejection creates an environment where you are starved for love or just don't fit in.

- When we feel rejected we tend to blame God for our looks, the color of our skin, our height, body shape, etc.

- Pride becomes a twin which says, "How dare they reject me!" OR, we have a sense of entitlement, complain and say, "I deserve better – I gave more, I did more, acknowledge me...!"

- Opinionated personality and the need to be right about things.
- Feelings of worthlessness, insecurity, or hopelessness.
- Seeking a parent's approval to feel loved or seeking others approval is a sign that you're basing your identity upon what they think of you.
- Envy, jealousy, and even hate can be rooted in rejection.
- Fear of confrontation (because your identity is based upon what they think of you).
- Stubbornness can also be rooted in rejection as well for this same reason. You have to be right, or else you feel worthless... that's because "who they are" (your identity) is based upon being right. This also ties in with opinionated personalities, who are always there to tell you about something, even if they have little or no real understanding to speak from.

- Pride can stem from a root of rejection. One of the things pride does-- is it causes you to move out of the timing of God with people, places and things. By doing so, you reject God's way, His word and His will for your life. When you know what's best for you outside of a Word of God or godly counsel, you have now rejected God because of pride.

Rejection also leads to being **performance oriented and driven (POD).** We perform so others can love and accept us. Certain variances can lead to OCD (obsessive compulsive disorder), where a person is basing their identity and who they are and how well they perform at something in life. At one time in my life (in the 90's) while seeing a Christian psychologist, I was diagnosed as one having OCD behavior. I was obsessed with being the best, being right, achieving the best grade, wearing the best, being seen in or with the best, going above and beyond to be liked or to please others...etc. Whenever we base who we are upon our performance, or our worldly knowledge or our giftedness, we are rejecting God who is our very present help. It is a blow to our true identity when we are always "reinventing ourselves" (another worldly term) to fit in and to please others. At one point in my life, I was playing the game in the 60's that asked the question, "*Will the REAL Rhonda stand up?*" Maybe you too are asking yourself this same question, because of rejection.

POD (performance oriented driven disorder), as it is termed, not only bases your identity and who you are or how well you perform at something in life, but it also causes you to focus and to become driven on having more, being more, desiring more. One is consumed with accomplishments, achievements, and what you have accumulated or what you have in life. The more you have, the more it validates who you are. You only feel accomplished, based on possessions, stuff, degrees, certifications, always a student. Shopping for clothes, shoes, purse fetishes... OCD personality, men/women - "love them and leave them" – the more the merrier... you get bored quickly. You look for the next thrill or natural man-made "high." You have to have the latest car, the latest haircut, the latest outfit - even if it looks horrible on you or even unbefitting for who you really are... you spend a whole lot of time trending or mimicking the world in lieu of being true to your true selves. The more you buy, the more degrees you possess, the more cars and shoes you have…. the more insatiable this spirit becomes (Boy, did I know a lot about that!!). You can also have unhealthy expectations based on the lives or lifestyles of others. Fear of failure. You are escaping to another place, another persona, and another world. Will the REAL YOU STAND UP?!! If you believe that your resume, the things you have done and accomplished must be impressive with hyped or exaggerated worldly things and accomplishments.

Ask yourself, when is the last time you obeyed Matthew 6:33 where God says, *"seek ye first the Kingdom of God"* instead of a desire to brand yourself as you spend a majority of your time building your own little kingdom... i.e. family, church, ministry, business, social network status/popularity... To whom you brand yourself becomes your master. If you are the master of your own fate, remember: we have been called to be bondservants to only one master - Jesus Christ.

Rejection causes us to be more carnal than spiritual. There is a way that seems right to man but in the end it leads to destruction (Proverbs 14:12). Many of our lives are being destroyed because we are chasing temporary highs, instead of flying high and being seated in heavenly places in Christ Jesus, with all these things we seek being placed in its proper order which is beneath us. Rejection is one of the main culprits that has robbed us and has stolen our identity. Know with assurance, that your identity can only be found in your relationship with Jesus Christ!

The good news is… if you fail to have acknowledged this trap before now, know that you are not a failure. If you blow it, catch the next breath of His wind. If you fall, you shall arise, and if you can only believe, then all things are possible! As you identify more with HIM and His word and not with them and the world, you too can begin to reject rejection.

Let Us Pray:

Father according to Your word In James 1:13-15 the bible addresses the roots of sin. Your word tells us that our sin, (which is ungodly behavior), is the result of our own lust enticing us to do something wrong. These lusts are listed in 1 John 2:15-16 as lust of the eyes, lusts of the flesh, and the pride of life. These learned behaviors that become practicing sins are rooted from rejecting who we are and who You have created us to be, as we have chosen to live in part or in full a fabricated life. This fabricated lifestyle has been created from a strong desire in pleasing others and ourselves more than a desire to please You. Lord, teach us how to love You more than we love ourselves. Forgive us for rejecting You. Forgive us for rejecting the plans and the purpose You have for us. Forgive us for rejecting ourselves. Forgive us for desiring to be more, want more, to accomplish and to do more, that is outside of Your will and timing for our lives. When we give in to these fantasies and temptation to please our own lusts, we mentally choose to reject and disobey You, God. Today, we denounce the hidden things and the visible things of dishonesty. We no longer want to be obsessed with finding our identity in the things of this world. We want to find our identity in You. In You we live and move and have our being. For we are Your offspring and not of our own. Create in us a clean heart and renew a right spirit within us. We choose to let this mind be in us which is also in Christ Jesus. As we seek You first and Your righteousness, give us as believers the mental toughness and capacity to make sound decisions and act on them with integrity, soundness and empower us with the ability to choose what is pleasing to You, God, as to annihilate the spirits OCD and POD behaviors biblically according to John 8:28-29; Philippians 4:13; Hebrews 11:6. Father today, we choose to reject rejection and no longer reject You. In Jesus' Name.

And it is so. Manifest! Amen.

Soul Session Scripture: *"Being in very nature God, did not consider equality with God something to be used to his own advantage; rather, he made himself nothing by taking the very nature of a servant, being made in human likeness. And being found in appearance as a man, he humbled himself by becoming obedient to death- even death on a cross! Therefore, God exalted him to the highest place and gave him the name that is above every name, that at the name of Jesus every knee should bow, in heaven and on earth and* *under the earth, and every tongue acknowledge that Jesus Christ is LORD, to the glory of God the Father."* Philippians 2:5-11

Soul Session Song: "Imagine me" by Kirk Franklin

Part Two - Rejecting Rejection - *Fixers*

There are those who struggle with rejection that also look for their identity in becoming what we call **"fixers."** A fixer is a person who is eager to tell everybody else how they need to be doing things. They tend to have all the answers, and they know what is right for everybody else, all the time! They find their identity in "believing" they are better than everyone else because they actually are good at fixing other people's problems! Fixers see themselves as some great wonder. Such a person attempts to be GOD in other people's lives, where they have no authority, but still will step right in as a "demigod." They want people to "worship" their abilities, their knowledge, their skills or their looks. They want or NEED to get the attention, the credit and the recognition. They see themselves as others salvation. They are the one person who can fix it. They are the Way, the

Truth and the Light. This person also operates in pride and has a God-like complex, again rejecting who they are and secretly desiring to be as God, which is Luciferic in nature (sounds familiar?).

Think about it, Lucifer is the first example of rejecting who you were created to be and to begin to look at yourself as being God. He loved the sound of his voice, as did others. He loved his looks, as did others. He loved his influence, as did others. So, it was not surprising that as he pondered on these things in his heart, he soon rejected who he was created to be and what he was created to do. As he became puffed up with pride in his heart because he was close to leadership and held an influential position, he was able to cause one-third of the angels to reject who they were and their created purpose, to fall from God's grace and get kicked out of heaven by ultimately rejecting God. The bible says that he, *"became so impressed with his own beauty, intelligence, power, and position that he began to desire for himself the honor and glory that belonged to God alone."* In other words, he rejected who he was and desired to be as God.

The truth is that we were all created for a purpose. It is in that purpose that we find our true identity and our godlikeness. But we will never be God, and never should we desire knowingly or unknowingly, try to take his place, in the lives of others he has created. Yet, that's what "fixers" do.

Rejection is an anti-Christ spirit because it opposes the very nature that God created in us. Each of us are to be loved, accepted, and appreciated. Rejection starves a person from love and from the acceptance that they were designed to receive. When we turn to others or even ourselves for love and acceptance, we are setting ourselves up for failure and the damage of rejection. Only God can be trusted as the true source of our identity. When we get to know God and His true nature; when we learn to love God… we now get to know and love ourselves. Jesus said, "My father and I are one" (John 10:30). This should be our number one goal in life. Then all other things will fall right into place. When you only do what you see you father do, say what you hear your father say… How can you then be confused in who you are?

Jesus came (for lack of a better way of saying it) to fix us! He accomplished His assignment by taking away the sins of the world and restoring us back to the Father. Instead of rejecting what He did for you and for others with a desire to be a fixer, allow what Christ did through His death, burial and resurrection to become your reality today. Surrender your heart and your mind and finally receive His forgiveness and grace, so the power to fix all things concerning you, can be released and revealed.

Let Us Pray:

I surrender to You today with all my heart and soul. Please come into my heart in a deeper way. I say, "Yes" to Your will and Your way and no longer to my own. Forgive me for trying to take Your place and exhort myself in others' lives as the one they need to turn to. I have struggled in finding my identity in my gifts and abilities to help and solve problems for others, but today, Holy Spirit, bring me to a deeper conversion to the person of Jesus Christ. I surrender all to You: my time, my treasures, my talents, my health, my family, my resources, my work, relationships, time management, successes and my failures. I release it and let it go. I will live for You and will not live to please and fix other people's problems. Jesus You are the problem -solver. You are the one they should turn to and not me.

I surrender my understanding of how things 'ought' to be and I surrender my will for Your will. I surrender to You the promises I have kept and the promises I have failed to keep with people. I surrender my desire to be god or the answer to the problem in anyone's life. I'm tired of being the fixer when obviously it's me that needs fixing. I surrender my emotions, my fears, my insecurities, my past and my present. I especially surrender _____ (Say the names of the people, places and things closest to your heart as they are revealed by Holy Spirit).

Lord, I surrender my whole life to You, my past, my present, and my future. I belong to You. I declare that I am a servant and not a savior.

And it is so. Manifest!

Note: Stay in His presence and listening for His voice. Let Him reveal what He needs to heal in YOU!

Soul Session Scripture: *"Finally, brothers and sisters, whatever is true, whatever is noble, whatever is right, whatever is pure, whatever is lovely, whatever is admirable- if anything is excellent or praiseworthy-think about such things."* Philippians 4:8

Soul Session Song: "I Surrender All" by William McDowell

Part Three - Rejecting Rejection - *Self-Rejection*

As we continue to connect the dots, **self-rejection** is another piece to this puzzle. Self-rejection is where a person rejects them self. They do not like who they are or even reject their race, culture or nationality. They are very critical of how they look, the shape of their body, the color of their skin, hair type or hair length. Most often their self-improvement plan is like one on steroids... always changing something about themselves (not for healthy purposes), but for vanity reasons seemingly to be accepted by others, but in reality, it is to be accepted by themselves. They never look good enough and are always finding something wrong with themselves. This often leads to self-hate, self-resentment, and unfounded jealousy of others, etc., and it is often tied in with self-unforgiveness. If the person has made mistakes in their life which they deeply regret, they live in condemnation, guilt and shame. They usually are oppressed and depressed, they will ESCAPE often in TV all day or sleep (induced by some over or under the counter narcotic, or they escape in other forms of feel good methods, sex, porn, food, alcohol, etc. Just as it hurts when others reject us, self-rejection can do more damage when we reject ourselves. What you are saying to God is that I reject how you created me. I don't like me and therefore I don't like you. Now you may not ever verbally say this to God, but this is what you are saying non-verbally. God, I hate the way you created me! If this is you, you need to denounce that verbal or non-verbal communication now!! If you are unhealthily overweight, then do something! If you want to live long and prosper - take care of God's temple. But if you are one who constantly for vanity sake need plastic surgery, tons of makeup to improve upon the look you want and not to enhance your true you... If you need a padded bra just because you feel you don't have enough breast — WHY? Who told you that?? Where did that come from? If you really believe blonds have more fun? Or redheads are sexy? Or only men with oversized muscles are real men? If only women with long hair are attractive or beautiful.... What does that say for the remaining ¾ of women in the world who may be natural, or don't want or can't afford "Remy" flowing down their back?!! If you're constantly dying your hair because you don't want to look or feel old. Those statements need to be readdressed, as you begin to understand that your belief system has been colored by the world's system and worldlier points of view. Re-evaluate what are you polarizing as beautiful or handsome and what is it based upon. When you look in the mirror can you identify with that same young girl or boy in a childhood picture? Do you even resemble her or him now? Or have you over the years tampered with the creator's creation so much, that you are not even recognizable based on HIS image of who you are? (ex. Michael Jackson) Listen... I don't have the answers to your questions, but concerning myself, I am willing to go to God and ask and where I need to deny myself to apprehend HIM and His thoughts concerning me. I am willing to do what I need to do to learn to love me without spending $300 or more a month just to FEEL PRETTY! Come on now... Even an unlearned child has to realize that something is wrong when half of my budget (and maybe even my tithe) is spent on enhancing my looks and not my life!

Then there's **perceived rejection**, where a person perceives something as rejection when it really isn't. For example, you walk into a room and someone turns and looks at you, turn back to look at the person they are standing with, and begin to talk. You believe that they are talking about you. You may say in your mind, "*Why is that person talking about me? She looked right at me and did not say anything, nor did she come over to talk to me. See, I knew she did not like me.*" Wow! This is the negative dialog perceived rejection causes. I recently was prompted by Holy Spirit to contact someone who attended an adult class I taught, someone I clearly acknowledged was offended. I reached out and attempted to apologize for anything that was perceived I said or did. In doing so, she let go of all the things she had been thinking... i.e.... She perceived I did not like her. She perceived I treated her different from everyone else in the class. She perceived I thought something which I did not. The more I tried to apologize, the more she told me what I did...YEARS

AGO!! After a while, I simply acknowledged her total recollection and account of the situations far outweighed my *"obvious"* lack of remembrance of those things. So again, I asked for forgiveness (I took the wrong regardless of what was perceived – because the Lord prompted me to call) – Obedience. Even though she said she forgave me a long time ago, it was clear she did not, and as Holy spirit said, she was offended. What she perceived was still in her heart and in her mind and apparently imbedded even in a false memory. Her perception of the memory of things, affected her paradigm. Until your paradigm shifts there is nothing you can do. At this point when you have done all you can, you stand on the Word that speaks of reconciliation. When you perceive rejection, remember it is your perception, don't judge others or the situation based on YOUR facts. Ask God to reveal the truth. Once you know the truth, PRAY and let God restore and reconcile your thoughts, patterns and behaviors to be more like His and not waste time responding to others based on their perception. An ideal way to cope with rejection is to always deflect and blame others. The bible says to pray for those who persecute you and speak all manner of evil about you

(Matthew 5:44) ... PRAY!!! Learn to love the unlovable for the sake of Christ. God loved you when you were unlovable and you had no clue you were living a lie, a false perception, even when you rejected Him, He still loved you. Let's follow His example.... So, when there was nothing else, I could do- - I did what the bible instructed, took the blame, forgave, and ... I prayed. Years had passed and this person moved away. One day, she reached out to me on Facebook to advise me that her mother died and asked for me to pray for her, "AND," would I call to pray with her personally. In her despair, God used that moment to reconcile the perceived rejection. God's Love Prevailed!

PERCEIVED REJECTION can be lethal!! I can drive someone to hurt others or hurt themselves. How does one convince the mind of anything opposite of what it believes? Only God can... and He will! We must pray against spiritual blindness of the eyes, mind and spirit, that accompany rejection wounds. People who are being controlled by spirits of rejection can talk themselves into believing that anything is true, when it is not. They will get offended, get angry and stay angry for years and sometimes forget even why. This spirit also distorts memories and causes forgetfulness. People (non- Christians and Christians alike) tend to receive perceived rejection easily because they do not feel good about themselves and many operate in insecurity and jealousy. Remember, the purpose of a spirit of rejection is to make us feel rejected. Perceived rejection can also cause a person to feel as if God has rejected them. This is a very common perception that I also encounter in the deliverance ministry.

Here is a biblical example of **perceived rejection**, which also causes feelings of envy, jealousy, and even hate to surface. This can be found in the story of King Saul and David:

*"And the women answered one another as they played, and said, Saul hath slain his thousands, and David his ten thousands. And Saul was very wroth, and the saying displeased him; and he said, they have ascribed unto David ten thousands, and to me they have ascribed but thousands: and what can he have more but the kingdom? And Saul eyed [literally meaning that he looked with jealousy upon] David from that day and forward. And it came to pass on the morrow [the next day, **that the evil spirit from God** came*

upon Saul, and he prophesied in the midst of the house: and
David played with his hand, as at other times: and there was
a javelin in Saul's hand. And Saul cast the javelin; for he said,
I will smite David even to the wall with it. And David avoided
out of his presence twice." I Samuel 18:7-11

First, we see the women praising David for slaying his ten thousand, and Saul for slaying his thousands. This perceived rejection made Saul angry with David, and jealous of him. When hearing this "HE THOUGHT" that David was out to take the kingdom from him. So, the very next day, an evil spirit came upon Saul and caused him to become exceedingly angry, to the point of attempting to murder David! Now that's some ugly fruit that all started with perceived rejection. It wasn't pride that opened Saul up to the evil spirit, but rather his reaction to his perceived rejection in his heart and mind.

The same is true when a person becomes stubborn or rebellious or has any other ungodly reaction to rejection. The rejection isn't the sin, but their reaction can be a serious sin. This can open the person to receiving unclean spirits and lead them down the path of destruction. God's Word puts stubbornness and rebellion, for example, in the same category as witchcraft and idol worship! *"For rebellion is as the sin of witchcraft, and stubbornness is as iniquity and idolatry. Because thou hast rejected the word of the LORD, he hath also rejected thee from being king"* (I Samuel 15:23).

Because Saul rejected the word of God; God rejected Him... Hmmm, what word of God are you rejecting or being disobedient to or rebellious of? Has God given you a specific word which you refused to do or believe because of your perception? Saying or Thinking - "I can't do that. I don't have a degree. I don't have the money or resources. They won't believe me. What if I lose my job? What if they reject what God told me to say?" ... It's a dangerous thing to reject the Word of God. When we do, we are rejecting God himself. He is His Word!

Today, if you find yourself rejecting God's Word or His instructions or being disobedient to the Word of God or His authority in God, harden not your heart. REPENT. Today is the day of your salvation. Let Him heal your misconceptions, self-rejection and perceived rejection. What God reveals; He wants to heal. It's time to reject Rejection!

Let Us Pray:

Daddy God…Abba Father, You know me. You know all about me. Please forgive me for looking for my identity in everyone and everything besides you. Forgive me for setting my heart on the things of this world, and for defining myself by other's words, opinions and earthly standards. I repent for spending a majority of my life, becoming a man-pleaser and not a having a stronger desire to please You. I repent from thinking on what is not of You; turning from Your words and holding on to another's words and opinions as if more important. Holy Spirit make known to me the reality of who my Father is, and who I am in Him. Send a burning discomfort to the areas of my life that are not in accordance with My Father's will, His Word and His Way. Today, I lay down all false identities that I have created, and in turn ask and receive mercy, grace and the freedom to do and be what You've created and called me to. Father, I find no hope or identity in my talents, skills or gifts. I find nothing redeeming in my race sex, beauty, looks, color, credentials. Awards, degrees, job title, familial, relational or ministerial position. None of these things can grant me a seat at Your table — Jesus, Your blood alone does that.

God, I find no peace in identifying with any movement, group, or person other than You. Let me find no rest apart from You. In You I desire to move, breathe and have my very existence. In You I am secure and made whole, righteous and blameless. In You I find purpose and joy because You are ever in me and by my side. Lord, thank You that I am precious, pursued, honored, dearly loved, wanted and cherished by You. In You, I am kind; I am patient and compassionate; I am gentle, and I am humbled to be a daughter or son of the Most High.

Father, I believe You are who You say You are; Help me I believe also I am who You say I am. For the doubt still lingering in my heart, give me faith. You are a faithful friend and a good, good Father, and I believe You will withhold no good thing from me, as I walk uprightly. I declare that I am a child of the Light, and today I will run and not grow weary.

And as I am set free, I will share the good news about Your love so other captives can be set free as we who once were broken, confused and lost are now reconciled and found. Beginning today, I will live in Your Presence and from the overflow of Your Holy Spirit, I will move. I know that You who have begun a good work in ME shall complete it even now, In Jesus' name.

And It Is So. Manifest!

Soul Session Scripture: *"I praise you because I am fearfully and wonderfully made; your works are wonderful; I know that full well."* Psalm 139:14

Soul Session Song: "You Know Me" by Steffany Gretzinger

Part Four - Rejecting Rejection - *Misplaced Identity*

In my studies, I began to ponder on where the root of rejection began. I was taken back in my thoughts (in Part One of this series) by Holy Spirit, I recalled in the Book of

Isaiah, where it speaks of one of God's three archangels named Lucifer.

"How you have fallen from heaven, morning star, son of the dawn! You have been cast down to the earth, you who once laid low the nations! **You said in your heart,** *'I will ascend to the heavens; I will raise my throne above the stars of God; I will sit enthroned on the mount of assembly, on the utmost heights of Mount Zaphon. I will ascend above the tops of the clouds; I will make myself like the Most High.' But you are brought down to the realm of the dead, to the depths of the pit. Those who see you stare at you; they ponder your fate."* (Isaiah 14:12-15)

The root of rejection is simply the negative seed planted that you ponder on in your heart (mind). This seed pondered on leads to the result of a **misplaced identity**. Lucifer had a misplaced identity. He believed he was God instead of an angel of God. He believed he could ascend to God's level through a lying spirit and a deceiving spirit. He believed he had the ability to make himself as the Most High God. Not only was he deceived and puffed up with pride, but his first root of sin was REJECTION! He was rejecting himself (what he was created to be) and by doing so, he rejected his Creator -God.

How many of us are rejecting ourselves and our identity, and trying to recreate who we are instead of who God made us? If you are doing so, you too are rejecting God. Whenever we base our identity on somebody or something other than what God or God's Word has to say about us, we make ourselves vulnerable to the damage of rejection. Many of us will base our identity on what our parents, family members, teachers, mentors, influential leaders, or friends think of us. These UGBs are a set up for Performance-Orientation bondages later in life because parents and others in our lives, often give **conditional love** based on our performance.

Let's go deeper... We may show our love under these conditions:

- Do well in school

- Play sports well

- Clean up or help around the house

- Cut the grass without being told to

- Make the Honor Roll

- Win awards in school, etc.

OR, I will also show my disappointment when these things do not occur. Hone in on the following questions. Ask yourself, what or who defines who you are and causes you to perform for fear of being rejected?

- Is it your job?

- Is it what your parents said or did to you?

- Is it what your friends think of you?

- Is it the opinion of others on how well you perform in the workplace?

- Is it based on your annual salary or how much money you have?

- Is it based on which your sorority or fraternity; organizations to which you belong?

- Is it what you think of yourself?

- Is it how physically strong, fit, fine or tall you are?

Now, think about this: When you die, will you want those things to continue to define who you are? Rising above rejection is all about what you base your identity upon. **The key to overcoming rejection is to solve the identity problem.** There are many sources for and of rejection; all human relationships are accompanied by the risk of rejection. Sometimes rejection comes during the school years. Perhaps you wore hand me-down clothes, you were of a different race, or you had a physical defect; so, you were singled out for ridicule at your school. Many people are disturbed by those who are different. If they do not know how to identify with you, they reject you.

If you are a person who is basing your identity on what your mother and father think of you, at any moment that any hint of disapproval comes from them concerning you, emotional hurt follows because they are the source of your identity. Anytime we base our identity on what we think of ourselves, or what others think of us; we virtually trust that person with our identity. Not even we are capable of truly determining who we are; only God is qualified for that job. That is why it is absolutely vital for us to understand the person that God has made in us, and who we are as new creations in Christ Jesus. We were never created to live apart from our Creator or base our identity His creation - this world.

Whenever we feel the hurt and pain from rejection, it's because our identity depends upon what that person thinks and/or says about us, that we believe to be true. If our identity didn't depend on what others think or say about us, we would be virtually immune from the damage that the spirit of rejection can cause. When our identity is based upon what the Word of God has to say about us, we now can become virtually rejection-proof. We can become immune from the wounds of rejection if we are not basing our identity upon what others think about us or even what we think of ourselves.

The closer a person is to you; the deeper their rejection can wound you. That's why those who are authority figures and influential in our lives are able to deeply wound you, because you look up to them and rely upon them. Parents often pass rejection on to their children when they say things such as, "I'm so proud of you!" But here's the catch. It is conditional. You only receive compliments when you get good grades or do something good. Conditional love causes feelings of rejection and bondages such as performance orientation and opens the door to a man-pleasing spirit. You are now driven to feel as though you must do better and be better to EARN your parents, spousal, children, coach or leader's validation or love.

Whether you like or dislike a person doesn't immune you from rejection. You can literally want to hurt or kill somebody, but still be affected by their rejection. Why? Because you are still looking to them for approval. You are basing your identity upon what they think of you You believe that their approval of you give your life meaning and purpose. Misplaced identity leads to a desire to please man more that it does to please God.

At a young or even an elderly age is when a person is vulnerable to rejection. Children are especially vulnerable to the damage rejection can cause because they are still developing their identity and learning about who they are. The elderly is also most vulnerable because their abilities and influence diminishes with time and with it their identity of who they once were and were capable of doing. Both the young and old are looking to be validated at both stages in their life.

For children, they see themselves in the eyes of statements like, *"you're too short, too tall, too fat, or too skinny. You have brown eyes when you should have blue eyes..."* You name it and kids will pick on it! Children can be very cruel and can cause so seemingly irreparable damage to other children through rejection. This is because their own identity is based on an identity crisis as well that is rooted in rejection. They do not know who they really are, or who they are called to be, so they go around putting other kids down to make themselves feel better. It's called bullying! Remember, small bullies end up being adult bullies too. But, if they knew who they were in Christ, it would be an entirely different story! They would as adults, seek to edify others, and help them find their identity and calling as well.

Is it possible to receive rejection from a child or even grandchild? Yes! Nobody is immune. This is simply an indication that you are basing your identity on what that other person thinks or says ... even if joking. You can be 100 years old and be damaged by the rejection of a caretaker, your spouse, your child and even your grandchildren. Rejection does not discriminate.

Speaking from a mother's point-of-view, there have been times that I felt rejected by my own children. Especially, if they said something that did not validate my being as "good" a mom as someone else. Even when I knew what to do was right concerning their welfare, that man-pleasing spirit will and can cause you to compromise and cause you to end up hurting them more than you would end up getting your feelings hurt. I have had to over the years apologize to my children for many things; and ask God to guide, shield and protect them emotionally, even if I was the conduit used to cause some of the challenges that I see in them today. Although you truly do not want to disappoint others, especially those closest to you, we should always strive to do the right thing, so God will be pleased. God should be more deserving of my love, honor and respect, than ANYONE else He also created.

~ We all need to Reject Rejection and lay down these fabricated and misplaced identities and strive to get our identity from God's Word! ~

It is vital that we base our identity upon what God's Word says about us. Let's learn the truth and stop focusing on the facts (the symptoms or voluntary actions). All things are subject to chain when we reject those Ungodly Beliefs. When we do, we become virtually immune from the devastating and hurtful effects of rejection that can come from having a stolen or misplaced identity.

So, what exactly does God's Word tell us about who we are in Christ?

➢ Because of God's great love for us, we are adopted into His family (1 John 3:1) and made joint heirs with Christ (Romans 8:17).

- ➢ We are made to sit in heavenly places [of authority over all demons, sickness, etc.] with Christ (Ephesians 2:6).
- ➢ We are blessed with all spiritual blessings in Christ (Ephesians 1:3).
- ➢ We are the righteousness of Christ through faith, thus being made right before God (Romans 3:22).
- ➢ We are entitled to a clean conscience before God because of the Blood and can have full assurance of faith when we go before Him (Hebrews 10:22).
- ➢ Our sins have been removed from us as far as the east is from the west (Psalms 103:12), and God Himself has chosen not to remember our failures (Hebrews 8:12).
- ➢ We are loved with the same love that the Father has for Jesus Himself! (John 17:23)

The Word of God is so rich and powerful in helping us define who we are in Christ. But having a father who committed suicide and a mother who I felt abandoned me by leaving this earth too soon (*wearing my emotions on my sleeve to reveal my truth*), there's one verse in Psalms that really puts the light on how I began to free myself from a misplaced identity and from the devastating effects of rejection: *"When my father and my mother forsake me, then the LORD will take me up."* (Psalms 27:10)

Tearing down the strongholds of rejection may appear hard, but it is as simple as merely receiving – with childlike faith – what God's Word has to say about your identity. He is your heavenly Father; He will never leave nor forsake you; Old things have passed away and now you are as a new creature in Christ, who is called to life, purpose, and meaning. You are His beloved. The apple of His eye. He loves you with an everlasting love. So, it does not matter how you feel. All that MUST matter is what God says... especially concerning you.

The wounds of rejection can open a person up to spirits such as abandonment, distrust, depression, worthlessness, self-centeredness, conceit, vanity or low-self-esteem to name a few. Those who have ongoing struggles with rejection should go through the deliverance process to have those spirits evicted (cast-out). There are often other bondages that result from rejection, some we have already named, but 'rebellious behavior' travels well with rejection.

Rejection is also an open door to a wide variety of bondages. Lack of love and rejection or abuse as a child, for example, can cause that child to turn to masturbation, pornography, fantasy sex and even the acceptance of Domestic Violence to fulfill their need to be loved. It can also cause unloving spirits, sexual identity crisis and sexual promiscuity, etc. (See Volume 2).

As with any abuse, but especially emotional, it's not so much the rejection that opens us up to unclean spirits, but rather our reaction to the rejection. This usually leads to the cover-ups, the lies, the masking, the false protection, which leads to a misplaced identity. These wounds of rejection must be healed, and my prayer has been that Soul Sessions Volume 1, is one tool that will help you to begin the healing phase and healing process.

It is imperative that you start seeing yourself for who you are in Christ, and the person that God has really formed within you. Your identity must come from your Creator and His manuscript that declares just what He thinks about you. He loves you with an everlasting love, and You are fearfully and wonderfully made. Printing out lists of Bible verses which speak of who you are in Christ and how much He loves you is vital in redeeming and restoring your true identity. Declaring the Word of God and daily affirming who you are in Him, is 'working out your own soul's salvation'. Since 'faith comes by hearing', reciting and memorizing to declare scriptures are incredible tools to help renew your mind and tear down these wicked strongholds that only want to rob you of your identity.

In the healing process of rejection, many times strongholds need to be torn down. I invite you to attend our God Encounters for deliverance and inner healing. Seek help from your Pastor or a spiritual leader that can help you walk through the process. Pray and ask God to lead you to a place or a person that can help facilitate your inner healing. Walk through the self-help worksheet located at the end of this book and remember, although the ministry we offer is only a phone call away, **GOD is just a prayer away**. He is the ultimate healer and He can and will (if allowed) restore your Identity in Christ.

Lastly, the Holy Spirit has shown me that whenever we feel the hurt and pain from rejection, it's because our identity depends upon what that person thinks of us. If our identity didn't depend on what others think of us, we would be virtually immune from the damage of rejection. That is why our identity must be based upon the Word of God, and what God has to say about us. His Word is the unshakable rock to which we need to build our house [OR LIFE] upon. I invite you today to Reject Rejection.

Let Us Pray:

Lord, I thank You making me aware of my identity in You. Thank You for giving me vision to see me as You see me and giving me a revelation of who I am in Christ. Help me to stand in Your truth and guard my heart with all diligence against every ungodly belief that has ensnared, trapped and tied me to the thought that I was rejected by others and by You. Help me to identify the lies of the soul ties and reveal any places where I am chained to the past in a negative way.

I repent of any lies of the past. [Name those lies and ask God to forgive you.] Teach me to hear Your voice and not believe the enemy's destructive lies about who I am. I thank You for my uniqueness and that I am made in Your image. I want to understand and feel the deep things in Your heart for me. I choose to believe the truth about how You see me. I thank You that I can hope, and a future filled with good and godly things. You have vision for my future. I can see clearly now. I shall live a fruitful life now that overflows with Your love to others. You have given me a greater authority in my prayer life. I want to continue to grow in the knowledge of who I am and come to know You on a deeper level. I no longer want anything to hinder my relationship with You.

- ➤ I thank You that [Say your name instead of "I"]:
- ➤ I am Your child (John 1:12)
- ➤ I have been justified (Romans 5:1)
- ➤ I am Your friend (John 15:15)
- ➤ I belong to You (I Corinthians 6:20)
- ➤ I am a member of Your body (I Corinthians 12:27)
- ➤ I have been established, anointed, and sealed by You (2 Corinthians 21-22)

- I am a citizen of heaven (Philippians 3:20)
- I am blessed in the heavenly realms with every spiritual blessing (Ephesians 1:3)
- I was chosen before the creation of the world (Ephesians 1:4; 11)
- I am holy and blameless (Ephesians 1:4)
- I am forgiven (Ephesians 1:8; Colossians 1:14)
- I am adopted as Your child (Ephesians 1:5)
- I have purpose (Ephesians 1:9; 3:11)
- I have hope (Ephesians 1:12)
- I am included (Ephesians 1:13)
- I am an overcomer (I John 4:4)
- I am protected (John 10:28)
- I am a new creation (2 Corinthians 5:17)
- I am qualified to share in Your inheritance (Colossians 1:12) I am the righteousness of God (2 Corinthians 5:21)
- I am kept in safety (I John 5:18)
- I am a citizen of Your Kingdom (Revelation 1:6)
- I can understand what Your will is (Ephesians 5:17)
- I have God's power (Ephesians 6:10)
- I am victorious (I Corinthians 15:57)

> I can do all things in Christ who strengthens me (Philippians 4:13)

Thank You for MY identity I have in You. Help me to live out this truth in my life every day. In Jesus' name, Amen.

Soul Session Scripture: *"For God so loved the world that he gave his one and only Son, that whoever believes in him shall not perish but have eternal life."* John 3:16

"Keep me as the apple of your eye; hide me in the shadow of your wings" Psalm 17:8

Soul Session Song: "How He Love Us" by Jesus Culture

Soul Session #8: To Be or NOT To Be
(Spirit of Indecisiveness)

Before the children of Israel crossed over the Jordan River to enter into their Promised Land, Moses stood on the mount as the spokesperson and Prophet of the Lord and said, *"Today I have given you the choice between life and death, between blessings and curses. Now I call on heaven and earth to witness the choice you make. Oh, that you would choose life, so that you and your descendants might live! You can make this choice by 1) loving the Lord your God, 2) obeying Him, and 3) committing yourself firmly to Him. This is the key to your life. And if you love and obey the Lord, you will live long in the land of Promise, that the Lord swore to give your ancestors."*

Decisions.........Decisions............Decisions!

There is a single mental move that each of us make daily, which in a millisecond, will either solve enormous problems or create them. It has the potential to improve almost any spiritual, personal or business situation you will ever encounter, or... it could literally propel you towards a path of seemingly failure and regret. This single most important mental move is called a Decision!

Decisions or the lack of them (indecisiveness) are responsible for the making, breaking or destroying of many lives, marriages, relationships, businesses and ministries. Believe it or not, those who know their God and hear His voice, obey His voice and a stranger's voice they do not follow (even if that "stranger's" voice happens to be their own).

There are those who are able to make good decisions. They are not easily influenced by the opinions of others but have decided to obey God's word and follow His plans for their lives. These are they, whose **"Success is NOT Negotiable,"** **but why do "they" look like the exception and not the** **norm?**

Anyone who has ever been caught in the Valley of Decision knows that indecisiveness can be very frustrating. Just thinking about what to do, can sometimes cause you to stress to the point of despair and even to the point of feeling sick. Whether the decision is BIG: Should I leave my job and start my own business? Should we purchase this house or relocate? Should I get married or divorced? Should I go to school or apply for this position? There are also those smaller decisions that can sometimes cause discomfort and frustration too? What should I wear today? Should I cut my hair or let it grow? Should I order french-fries or mashed potatoes as my side dish? Should I attend this event by myself or with a friend? Then, there are other decisions that we have made "IMPORTANT" ... Who do I "add" as my Facebook friend? Who do I follow on twitter? What picture do I post on Instagram? What TV shows do I watch tonight? Even these miscellaneous indecisive moments can become borderline obsessive as you click through channels wasting time; or stand in front of your refrigerator staring at its contents; or spending time deciding what to post on social media; or you choose to change clothes 10 times before deciding what to wear; or you hold up the drive-through line, while deciding which side order you want to eat with your chicken. DECISIONS!!!!!

As informed consumers, we have come to expect a variety of choices... and every day we are faced with a plethora of choices to choose from. It is estimated that an adult makes about 35,000 remotely conscious decisions each day. This number may sound absurd, but in fact, and as your level of responsibility increases and circumstances change, so does the smorgasbord of choices you are faced with.

You and I have been given a free-will and a multitude of choices in life about:

- what to eat
- what to wear
- what to purchase
- what we believe
- what jobs and career choices we will pursue
- how we vote
- who to spend our time with
- who we will date and marry
- what we say and how we say it
- whether or not we would like to have children
- what we will name our children

> who our children spend their time with

> what they will eat, etc.

Each choice carries certain consequences - good or bad. The ability to choose is an incredible and exciting power that we have each been entrusted with by our Creator and for which we have an obligation to be good stewards of. But are we?

Decision-making moments will consume your thoughts until you choose one outcome over the other. And, even after you make a choice, many still obsess with, *"Did I make the right decision?"* Your thoughts then continue to harass you as you worry whether you made the right decision over and over again. Now enters the vicious cycle that includes the opinions of men. While the scripture does state that there is safety in the multitude of counselors, many choose to speak with those that are more than likely your influencers. If so, in this process you will depend on them to basically make the decision for you. The viciousness of this cycle created from this form of indecisiveness is that, if it works out, they will always want the credit for the outcome, and if it does not work in your favor, you will eventually blame them for the choice that determined the negative outcome.

The decision to leave Egypt after 400 years of captivity caused Moses to become the object of the Children of Israel's viciousness when they thought their freedom was threatened. In Exodus 14:10-11 TLB we read, *"As the Egyptian army approached, the people of Israel saw them far in the distance, speeding after them, and they were terribly frightened and cried out to the Lord to help them. And they turned against Moses, whining, 'Have you brought us out here to die in the desert because there were not enough graves for us in Egypt? Why did* **you** *make us leave Egypt?'"* Even though we know that was not the case, the blame game is often played when the advice or influence of others does not turn out as desired or expected. I've often wondered that if this pattern of indecisiveness by the children of Israel could be a reason they could not enter into the promised land. They never believed what God promised!

It's always easier to blame others for our inability to trust God and have faith. This doublemindedness often prevents us from receiving what God has promised and leaves us with hurts, disappointments and setbacks in life. The intimacy of your relationship with God, the health of your mind and body, the well-being of your family, your marriage, your social life, your business or ministry and even the type of relationships you develop, are all dependent upon your ability to make sound decisions.

The power of a decision is seen throughout the scripture from the very beginning when God decided to design creation and to make man. When Jesus made a decision to say, 'Not my will but your will be done!' When Judas decided to betray Jesus for 30 pieces of silver, and when Mary said, "*Be it unto me according to your word.*" Decision making is something you cannot avoid. NOT to make a decision, is evident that you just made one! You can virtually eliminate conflict and confusion in your life by becoming proficient at decision making.

You would think that anything as important as decision-making, when it has and hold such far-reaching consequences and power would be taught in every home or school... but it's not! And to compound the problem, not only is decision-making missing from the curriculum of our educational institutions, it has also been absent from many corporate trainings, most service industry programs, are just a one-pager of information for employees to read, until recently. It has also been strange to me that this subject is not being taught in our religious institutions or churches; and yet, for many of our spiritual leaders the balance of a person's soul (life) has been placed in their ability to make God decisions and good decisions. It is automatically believed that since a person is a spiritual leader they know how to make sound decisions, but we have learned that this is not true with everyone. One word from God can change a person's life. But what about that one word NOT from God, that also changes the person's life in a negative way? How many wrong decisions were made by parents, teachers, mentors, etc., that has had internal ramifications, that now has wounded others. Yet every day, every hour, every minute, leaders from all walks of life are expected to make sound decisions. When the word "soundness" is even subjective.

When we are disciplined in our thoughts and corresponding actions, our daily decisions will bring order to our minds and of course, this order is then reflected in our life, our home, in our business, ministry and in our relationships. The cardinal principle of immediate decision making is DECIDE RIGHT WHERE YOU ARE, with what information you have, amidst any and all circumstances you are facing to: *TRUST in the Lord with all your heart* (soul, mind, will, emotions, experiences, dreams, hopes), *and lean not to your own understanding* (reasoning, intellectual thoughts, facts, reality, experiences, perceptions). *In all your ways* (conduct, attitudes, behaviors, traditions, customs, methods), *acknowledge Him* (surrender to; recognize; adhere to; confer with; obey) *and He will direct your path* (the path of life, affairs of life; life circumstances and situations you face, your very way of life).

When I was a Law Enforcement Officer, we had this exercise called 'Shoot or Don't Shoot'. Each officer would be placed in a simulated street situation where they would need to respond with the appropriate level of force based on the scenario created with pop-ups. The decisions you made in a split-second determined life or death; not only for you but could also result in the wrongful death of someone innocent or the justifiable death of a person who posed an imminent threat with the use of deadly force. Back in the 80's, there was a low percentage of officers who did not pass this exercise in the number of times required. Those who could not effectively make the right decision, as well as those who made no decision and ended up "dead," subsequently were not hired. Some decisions cannot be corrected or changed. You don't get a do-over in life, as you would in a simulated exercise. The choices we make are important. If the wrong decision is made, the consequences can be detrimental for you and for others. Based on what's going on today, decisions made by law enforcement, politicians, CEOs, cleric, educators, etc., are very costly; and they are affecting whole communities and a nation at large. *(I don't know if they still have this training for local law enforcement officers today, but if not, they should...hmmm).*

And what about the person who makes a decision to drive drunk and kill a mother, leaving her three children motherless. Or someone's daughter, who is date-raped at a frat house because five boys decided to join in for what they call fun. Or the husband that decides to take out his frustration on his wife until she's hospitalized. Or the child who is paralyzed by a stray bullet of a gang's senseless shooting spree. Or a young boy going to the store for skittles and ends up dead. These decisions are those meant to kill, steal and destroy. If these type decisions are prevalent in your home or community, then do not just hear the news, lock your doors, and remain on the fence of neutrality or indecisiveness concerning these grave issues; you need to make a decision now to begin to pray.

In 1 Samuel 30 we find David and his men coming home to a city that was burned down and all their women and children were kidnapped. The bible says, after they could weep no more, the people then decided to turn on David and begin to speak of stoning him. David was very distressed, but he first decided to encourage himself in the Lord. Secondly, David not knowing what to do, decided to

PRAY and ASK the LORD for guidance and direction. By deciding to ask God to weigh in first on such an important decision, God honored him by telling him to go and recover it all. So, thirdly, David followed the Lord's instructions, and all was recovered and forgiven.

So, the question is, "When you are making your decisions are you 1) trusting, 2) leaning, 3) acknowledging, and, 4) surrendering to the plan, purpose and will of God," as stated in Proverbs 3:4-6? Do you PRAY first and ask God for guidance, directions and clarity as David did in 1 Samuel 30? Do you take the time to think, WWJD? What Would Jesus Do? Then follow His example.

Now...I know that sounds corny, but believe me, during the times that I have stopped and pondered that thought WWJD...then decided to respond accordingly and obediently, everything turned around for my good. Doors opened that no man could close. Ways were made out of no way. Favor untold met me at the point of my need. When I decided to trust Jesus and not in myself, my husband, my pastor, my banker; or in friends or relatives or even in the government; somehow I knew all things were working for my good. Only when my decision ultimately was based on the Word of God or derived from the Wisdom of God, the Heart of God or through the means of prayer, was I able to move beyond appearances and establish God's will for myself in the earth by making a decision that did not cause conflict between my spirit and my soul.

So, the decisions we as Christians make should be based on the principles that are designed to create winning opportunities. Those that will allow God's glory and honor to fill the earth to be seen by mankind! This in return, will lead to DECISIONS by mankind, to want to become acquainted with our God and the hope that is given to all that will trust and obey. Now, I can give you a plethora of biblical examples of this very thing, but today I have **DECIDED** to make this a more practical soul session and give credit to a few examples of those who practiced the principles of faith and tapped into the laws God has placed in this earth realm for those who will make a decision to only believe. Laws when put into motion, work both for those who know God and those who have yet to confess their acknowledgment of God! Laws or Principles in this earth are universal. Like sowing and reaping!! If you sow money you will receive money. If you sow kindness, you will reap kindness. If you sow positive words, you will reap positive results. No matter what, if you have faith and believe what you say, then you WILL have what you say! Good or Bad, the decisions you make will frame your world with limitations or possibilities. The choice is yours! Today, you too can call those things that be not as though they are; and if you do not doubt in your heart, you shall have or produce by choice, what you have decided to believe and to say. And believe it or not, this principle works for anyone!

I read the story that detailed that when then President John F. Kennedy asked Werner Von Braun what it would take to build a rocket that was able to carry a man to the moon and return him safely back to earth; Werner Von Braun's answer was simple and direct, **"the will to do it."** The bible says, *"if you are willing and obedient you will eat the good of the land"*. (Isaiah 1:19)

President Kennedy never asked 'IF' it was possible. Because, ALL things are possible for those who believe!! Nor did he ask 'IF' they can afford it! Why, for where there is vision there will always be Provision! **President Kennedy simply made a decision to go for it and** said, "I will put a man on the moon and return him safely to earth before the end of the decade." That fact that it had never been done in history was not even taken into consideration. He decided where he was, with what he believed; and what he had. What did he have? ... A God-inspired idea. He had a dream! So did Dr. Martin Luther King, Jr. MLK had a dream...and sometimes decisions you make for the dream can cost you everything. He knew and stated, that he was not going to make it into the "Promised Land" just like Moses. But with boldness and confidence after stating he would not get there with us, he still made a DECISION to go all the way. He knew just like Jesus that his decision had the power to change the whole world as we knew it. And boy.... did it!

The objective was accomplished in President Kennedy's mind, the moment he decided. The dream that Martin Luther King saw and decided to release was fulfilled the moment he released it. It was only a matter of time… (which is governed by natural laws) before his decision spoken into existence, would line up with the spiritual law that set it in motion - a Decision. Heaven's decree waiting to be established.

His decision to believe it could be done, was made possible by his faith in the decision he made. By his resolve, things came into being. The invisible soon became visible! Soon, the end-goal was manifested for the whole world to see, just because they decided to believe and therefore spoke. When God decided to create you, He knew you were able to do all that He created you to be and do. He has so much faith in His decision that soon, the invisible will also become visible for the whole world to see. The question is today, will you decide to believe God concerning the greatness that is inside of you? Or will you live life in disbelief because of something you did instead of the someone you are? I encourage you right now, to decide to Have Faith In God concerning you.

Anyone who has ever studied on great thinkers know that they are also great result-oriented goal-getters too! Why? Because they are not afraid to take a risk to make sound and yet faith-filled decisions. Your thoughts ultimately control every decision made. Some decisions we make daily are subconscious, i.e. To run away from a fire. To go inside or seek shelter if there is a thunderstorm. To put cream or not in our coffee (smile). You do what you subconsciously think more than what you consciously believe you think. You are the sum total of your thoughts. You have framed and designed your world with everything you have decided to believe in in your subconscious thoughts. Every decision you've made was decided upon your preconceived, subconscious or conscious thoughts. And, as a man thinks in his heart, so is the man. By asking the Holy Spirit to lead and guide you to all truth, you can exercise the faith needed to tear down those ungodly belief systems we have decided to believe and acquire the mind of Christ as we choose to change our world while making good and godly decisions. Especially the IMPORTANT ones we will make. We need to intently discipline ourselves to not only make decisions that are sound, prudent, wise and those that would please God, but also those that can affect positive change for others.

The greatest stumbling block you will ever encounter when making important decisions in your life is CIRCUMSTANCE. We let circumstances get us off track and then block us from moving forward into the "land of promise." We are then as the Reubenites. This is the Tribe of Israel that decided to stay on the east banks of the Jordan in the wilderness instead of crossing over into the Promised Land. More dreams are shattered and goals unfulfilled because of life's seemingly impossible circumstances, that causes us to stay and never move forward. We look at our circumstances which seem greater, become indecisive, and miss opportunities. Certainly, being unable to make a quality decision based on circumstances is frustrating for the indecisive person, but, being indecisive also affects those around you. Many people: your spouse, children, family, coworkers, and friends are all influenced by your decision-making or lack thereof. Your wavering decisions may be overcome by someone else's quick thinking, or you may be so distracted by the very thought of what to decide and lose track of when to do it, that it can then become costly, i.e. higher interest rates, airline ticket price changes; deadlines to register or apply; missed opportunities; or late replies to important emails, to name a few.

Being unable to decide happens to the best of us. But when being indecisive begins to become more of a regular occurrence than a rare one, your relationships, your career, your finances, your ministry, and your health, can suffer. Indecision is a silent killer of opportunities and dreams. So, when you are facing those IMPORTANT decisions, that do NOT need to be made at that very moment, do not allow stress and fear to overtake you emotionally.

Here are a few tips on how to make tough and costly decisions:

- PRAY first...Be anxious for nothing! (Philippians 4:6) Ask for the wisdom of God (Proverbs 4:7 - Getting wisdom is the wisest thing you can do! And whatever else you do, develop good judgment.)
- Realize you have as much time as you will need. Do not allow pressure or the tyranny of urgency to

overwhelm you. Acknowledge that God is in control and not you.

- List your options. Write down all the possible outcomes of your decision.

- If necessary, gather information that will help determine your decision. Separate the facts versus fiction. Research the pertinent facts. Ask family and friends who have experience in helping you to make this decision or ask those who are mature, honest, wise and unbiased for input, BUT not a decision.

- Determine your absolutes and your desired outcomes. What will you accept and what is unacceptable. What is negotiable and then put aside what about this decision is not negotiable.

- Meditate on the desired outcome. See it before you see it. How does it feel? What does it look like? Who are you sharing the moment with? Are you happy with your choice?

- Now determine, if you take a RISK (faith) what is the worst-case scenario? Can you live with it? Can you still praise God? (Example: Three Hebrew boys).

- When at peace with the various outcomes of the risk, thank God in advance and make your decision!

Listen, God has made us more than able and qualified to make decisions when we yield to the leading of the Holy One who lives on the inside of us. How often have you heard yourself saying, I would like to do this or have this, but I can't because-----? Whatever follows after because----- is YOUR seemingly insurmountable circumstance. Circumstances cause detours and delays in your life, but you should never permit them to stop you from making right or important decisions that can also change the circumstances and situations in your life and ultimately in the lives of others. When the weight of the circumstance outweighs your expectation in your dreams and your vision, it will always override your decision to agree with what God has a desire for you to have or accomplish in this life.

If every time we made a decision a hand from heaven came down to point us in the right direction, we would have no need to develop our god-like abilities to make right decision. God does help lead the way, but when it comes to decision making, He guides us through His word and wisdom by His Spirit. God will always place us in teachable moments to listen, trust and obey. To hear His voice and not that of a stranger, even when that strange voice or opinion can come from within ourselves.

When the time comes, we will either choose the right path or suffer from the consequences of a wrong decision. When you follow His words, you can never be sent in the wrong direction. The bible says to, *"Trust in the LORD with all thine heart; and lean not unto thine own understanding but in all thy ways acknowledge Him, and He shall direct thy paths."* The key to making right decisions is relying on God's wisdom and not the wisdom of man or your own.

Below are 8 Bible verses of wisdom that can be used for making the right decisions:

> *"If any of you lacks wisdom, you should ask God, who gives generously to all without finding fault, and it will be given to you."* (James 1:5)

➤ *"Call to me and I will answer you and will tell you great and hidden things that you have not known."* (Jeremiah 33:3)

➤ *"For the Lord gives wisdom; from His mouth comes knowledge and understanding."* (Proverbs 2:6)

➤ *"The heart of a man plans his way, but the Lord establishes his steps."* (Proverbs 16:9)

➤ *"And your ears shall hear a word behind you, saying, 'this is the way, walk in it,' when you turn to the right or when you turn to the left."* (Isaiah 30:21)

➤ *"Do not be anxious about nothing, but in everything by prayer and supplication with thanksgiving let your request be made known to God."* (Philippians 4:6)

➤ *"Finally, brethren, whatever is true, whatever is honorable, whatever is right, whatever is pure, whatever is lovely, whatever is of good rapport, if there is any excellence and if anything, worthy of praise, dwell on these things."* (Philippians 4:19)

> *"You shall decide and decree on something and it shall be established."* (Job 22:28)

Moses told the children of Israel to decide to go in and take the land, so that they could represent the Lord in a foreign land. In other words, they decided to represent the Lord in a foreign land, but yet, it was the same land that they were promised. You and I have been commissioned to represent the Lord and let our light so shine that when men see us, they see Christ. We stated when we accepted Christ as our Lord and Savior that we too, as the children of Israel, would make the choice or decided to:

1) Love the Lord our God with all our heart mind soul and strength;

2) Obey Him (obedience is better than any sacrifice we could ever make) and,

3) Commit yourself firmly to Him. You must decide to commit your life and your work to the Lord, so He can establish it!

This is the key to OUR life. We MUST **DECIDE** to "love and obey the Lord, and we will live long in the land of Promise that the Lord swore to give your ancestors." Today I decide to *"Seek first the Kingdom of God and His righteousness and then all these things I desire will be added unto me."* Today I decide to choose God... I decided to choose Christ above all! Now, what do you decide?

Closing Decision:

If you have yet to decide to make the Lord Jesus Christ, the Savior of Your life, do not remain in the Valley of Indecision. God has been too good to you for you to stay neutral. The fight between good and evil is quite evident and is very noticeable in what is going on in our world today, in our city or community today; even in our home today. I invite you to way out your options, even using the tips given above. There is no doubt in my mind, that you too will come to the same conclusion as I did and decide that there is no safer place today than to be in a relationship with Jesus Christ. No one will ever love you more than Our Heavenly Father. He knew you were going to read this today and has been waiting on you to decide here and now to join the family of God. What more will you decide to lose by not making a decision to immerse yourself in the love, grace and mercy of our Heavenly Father? If you have decided to allow Jesus Christ to live in you and with you, read and pray the prayer below..... Then once said, you must tell someone. You can email us and let us know.

Dear God, I know that I am a sinner and there is nothing that I can do to save myself. I confess my complete helplessness to forgive my own sin or to work my way to Heaven. I need You in my life for it to have true meaning. I admit I have been doing things my way. Sometimes I get it right, but most of the time I still end up making a mess of things and I need Your wisdom. I really need You. I'm tired of doing things my way and on my own. Today, I have decided to ask You to help me do it Your way. I invite You to invade my situation and circumstances by coming into my life and become my Savior and My Lord. Help me Lord to forgive anyone who has hurt me, so I can be forgiven (If there is anyone call out their name). Now Father, because I do believe that Jesus Christ came and died for my sin and was raised from the dead as a guarantee for me, I ask You to please forgive me of my sin and grant me repentance. Come into my life and fill the longing I have for someone greater than me to consume me. Fill this emptiness within me with Your Holy Spirit. Take control of my life as I offer myself as a living sacrifice. Help me to love You greater than I love myself and others. Help me to trust You and to live my life for You starting now. Help me to truly understand Your grace and Your mercy. Let Your will be done in my life from this day forward. I am grateful that You have promised to receive me despite my many faults, sins and failures, but as of today these things are no longer held against me. Father, I take You at Your word and I thank You that You are my Savior and my Lord. Thank You for the assurance that You will walk with me every day of my life. Thank You for hearing this prayer and I declare with certainty that I am now saved. In Jesus' Name.

And it is so. Manifest! Amen.

Welcome to the Family...... All Sin and Soul Ties Gone! Now, this is the Greatest Soul Session of ALL!

Note: If you've made this decision, please email us at rfl@thewinningimage.net. We will reach out and send you information to make other great choices and decisions. RWFL

Soul Session #9: Breaking Ungodly Beliefs and Unhealthy Soul Ties (Prayers of Renunciation - Detoxing the Soul)

Prayer: (Self-Help Deliverance)

*Jesus Christ, I confess that You are the Lord of my life and that You alone hold the highest position of **power** and **authority** under our Father's throne. I proclaim that You, Jehovah, are my Spiritual Father, and that Your throne holds **all** power, **all** authority and rules over **all** powers and principalities.*

*Father, I acknowledge and am in agreement with all Your ways. I am in **full** agreement with the position You have given Jesus Christ as Lord over my life. I sit myself at Jesus Christ's feet, under the truth of His teachings, and I surrender and yoke myself to the mantle of His rule and power. I renounce sin, Satan, his works and all of his minions of deceptive trickery which comes against the believer, and the unbeliever.*

Through ignorance I had walked a sinner's walk and had talked the language that sinners speak before I came to accept Jesus Christ into my life. I had indulged myself with sinful behavior because I did not fully understand or appreciate the love You have for me. I not only ask for your forgiveness, but in my desire to truly be free; I ask that you grant me repentance.

(If there is anything you are led to speak out and repent of, do so now. Repentance work should be done before embarking upon seeking the change this book has been written to do. Take as long as you need before moving on.)

In Jesus Christ's name, Father, I proclaim this day to be a day of washing sin from my life and a day of severing unhealthy soul ties from people who I know have doors open to sin, and who affect me because they do. I pray for a washing of the blood of Jesus Christ over me, and for Holy Spirit to uproot and sever from me every cord that Satan has attached to me from these people, to cause a work of oppression because of my association, former agreement, or what appeared to be my agreement for another person's sin. Amen.

For any person who has not had sexual encounters before marriage, or who has never entered into an intimate relationship, you can skip over this part. *

Father, I repent for having had sexual relationships before marriage. I seek Your forgiveness, Father, for every time I sinned in this way, for I know this type of behavior does not reflect Your character. By the Blood of Jesus Christ, I speak to break off of me every negative and spiritually dangerous connection my soul has made to each one of those sexual partners. Let their sins be theirs and my sins be mine and covered under the blood of Jesus Christ.

Father, if any one of these ex partners has sinful behavior in their life, or are living in disobedience to Your ways, I want to clarify that I am not in agreement to any of their sinful ways, or disobedience. In the name of Jesus Christ, I ask that God, Jehovah's Warrior Angels, take their swords and completely sever each and every type of soul tie and attachment that has been connected to me from each of those sexual partners, in that I do not take on any

consequence to their sins, or any consequence from my prior
involvement with them.

(If you feel led, or the Holy Spirit brings anything to remembrance that you need to forgive, or seek forgiveness for regarding an ex-partner, or you feel led to repent or renounce anything regarding them, do so now before continuing for repentance and forgiveness leads to freedom.)

Instruction

Here is where you need to name the people, groups and situations that you realize are causing you (or may cause you) spiritual upset through a spiritual connection to them. This is also where you realize the need to renounce, break and rectify this spiritual upset through the blood of Jesus Christ.

Here is where you also need to name the specific SOUL-spirits (i.e. depression, unforgiveness, indecisiveness, deceitfulness, ungodly belief...) that has tied itself to your soul, and is intertwined in your thoughts, decisions, actions, and situations. A soul-spirit that you realize is causing you (or may cause you) spiritual upset through a spiritual connection to them, and where you realize the need to renounce, break and rectify this spiritual upset through the blood of Jesus Christ

Take a moment and think of any person, or group or spirit who you were once associated to and who you know had embraced a sinful way of living; who generates discord, heaviness, deception, false doctrine and upset to others. Individuals who are/were involved with occult activities, or who you know are involved with **anything** that you know **(or have good intuition)** is un-Godly.

Anyone you have had a falling out, disagreement or break up with, and in which there were hard feelings, or mean spiritedness projected against you. Recount any group, club, organization, gang, brother/sister hood that have un-Godly beliefs and which had you make unholy vows, or oaths.

These are negative spiritual soul ties that need to be broken. These are individuals who you:

1 – If you once (or still do) had some form of association/agreement with, or appeared to be in agreement with, and what Satan is using as a loophole against you to make you an accomplice to their sins by association because you had never officially rescinded (through the blood of Jesus Christ). Whatever association, agreement, appearance of agreement, or involvement you may have had for them, their beliefs, or their sins before must be addressed and renounced explicitly.

2 – A person, or group, whom you had a bad experience with and where that person, (or group of people) holds, or may hold condemnation toward you.

If you are recognizing several people, groups, spirits or situations to sever soul ties with, do so now – one at a time.

Name the *person, group, spirit, gang, sisterhood or brotherhood* etc., you want dealt with, and speak out the situation of what makes that person, or group, or spirit groupings spiritually dangerous to you and speak forth the breaking of that agreement that once was. There are some different examples at the end of this prayer that might give you a better idea of how you may want to pray for each individual situation.

Speak forth every person, group of people, or spirit you feel led to be specific in severing associations with, or to put a distance between you and their sins and your sins. Then continue reading prayer.

*In the name of Jesus Christ, I speak forth my release from **every form of** spiritual attachment, cord, yoking, spiritual oppression, curse and condemnation that had formed and connected itself to me because of a broken friendship, negative soul tie, traumatic abuse, physical/emotional oppression, or an association to a spiritually dangerous person.*

*In the name of Jesus Christ, I recant every un-Godly vow I had ever spoke at any time in my life, and I speak forth my release from every un-Godly vow I had ever made, or which anyone else may have spoken regarding me. I command that all negative spiritual influences that are operating against me be **nullified** and **detached** from me this very moment. In the name of Jesus Christ, I **cancel** the assignments which Satan has given to each demonic spirit to work against me.*

*I **bind** and **rebuke** each demonic spirit that was assigned to enforce spiritual attachments against me, and I **command** that each and every one of these demonic spirits be cast out and sent to dry places now, at this very moment.*

Father, I pray that Your gifts increase in my life, especially the gift of discernment. Holy Spirit, please help me to recognize when a person becomes spiritually dangerous to me because of sin in their life and help me to be wise in how I will deal with that. Help me to discern when a fellow Christian is not taking their walk in the Lord seriously, is living more for the world than they are obeying the Word and living for the Love of You. Help me to discern when, and the courage to walk away from believing things I or they shouldn't; such as false doctrinal beliefs, cult like ideas, etc., and again, give me the wisdom and the boldness to know what to say to these people to distance me from their sins, behavior or negative influences.

In Jesus Christ's name, I Praise You God and give You the Glory for breaking Satan's legal rights to me because of an unhealthy spiritual tie that was formed between myself and another person, or group of people or demonic spirit that satan was using against me to kill, steal and destroy. I thank You, God, for removing the blinders, healing the soul wounds, cutting the ties, and setting me free from the oppressions and demonic influences themselves.

I believe and therefore I speak. And it is so. Manifest!

Give God your praises and reflect on what He has just done for you in setting you free. Some people may not feel the connections severed, or chains broken, or oppression lift as well as other people will — but trust me when I say they are indeed broken spiritually by Faith. BUT faith without works leaves unresolved issues. We now must learn to guard our heart (soul), for out of it will flow out the same issues. So.... Are you ready now to do the works? There may be people you need to go to forgive or some you may need to disconnect from or set healthy boundaries. Either way, *"As it is in heaven, let it be in earth (in YOU) and on earth (in your environments)."*

Congratulations! You have decided to embrace the THOUGHT that you **can be and do** whatever you **IMAGINE.** You decided to **Untie Your Soul**! Embarking upon this quest demonstrates your desire and determination to be **transformed,** first and foremost, by **renewing your mind**. You must realize that your outer expressions and actions are only the results of inward reflections. You are the sum total of your thoughts.

"Sooner or later, those who WIN are those who THINK they can!" Richard Bach

A successful life is always under construction. We will not be complete until we see HIM as He is...But, we are houses not built by Man, and the blueprint of our destiny has all the building materials needed within to erect the winning image...the IMAGE and LIKENESS of God. And although As HE is So are We, in this world NOW, when we combine our distorted IMAGE with our erroneous THOUGHTS, with learned behaviors that are not Christ-like, our performance in life appears mediocre and unsuccessful. But now that we have:

"Changed Your IMAGE, (you can) Change Your PERFORMANCE." EJ McKenzie

You may still see yourself as average or even below average. You may think that your windows of opportunities to achieve greatness are closing or have closed and your timeline to become successful in whatever you desire has passed you by. What you SEE will cause you to SAY Words that will eventually frame your world. You are the sum total of what you see internally. Believe, agree with, and then SAY! For in the beginning God said, and it was! TODAY, I'm asking that you look within and SEE the wellspring of success, wealth and prosperity, deeply embedded with unlimited possibilities waiting for you to simply SEE, BELIEVE, AGREE and SAY, **WHAT GOD SAYS!**

Did you know that men were born to succeed and not fail? *So*, say this with me…. "There is no Failure in God and therefore there is no failure in me". Let's find out how this could possibly be true in today's FINAL "*Soul Session in Volume 1 - Healing for the Soul.*

Soul Session #10: What's In Your Hand? (Spirit of Faith)

Have you ever thought or said to someone else, "**IF** things were different, I could really succeed... **IF** I had a job or a better job; **IF** I had a better education; **IF** I had a thousand dollars or a million dollars. **IF** I were born rich; **IF** I was married or **IF** I was single! **IF** I had transportation; **IF** I wasn't in foreclosure or tied down to this mortgage for the next twenty years; "**If** only I had this, or **if** only I had that". **IF** I didn't have to work! **IF** only we weren't in a recession!!! Notice the common thread of failure, is the WORD "**IF!**"

IF, represents a WORD filled with excuses... in a world filled with unlimited possibilities. Your situation today is no different than those who have decided to not allow the **IF factor** to determine their destiny. Instead they have decided to allow the GOD in them to prove that He is bigger than "**IF**" and that **HE is more than enough!**

"**WHAT IF**" you stopped waiting for things to get better, before you made them better. "**What IF**" you revisited your dreams and your ideas and stepped out in faith. "**What IF**" you decided to create a solution to the problem. **"What IF"** you allowed your gift to make room for you in your area of interest, expertise or passion. **"What IF"** you decided you were healed, in spite of what the doctor said. **"What IF"** you actually believed what you prayed. **"What IF"** today you decided to experience the perfect WILL of God for your life, your marriage, your relationships, your family, your business, your ministry... **"What IF!"**

First you must recognize that YOU HOLD the power to do something with your life, regardless of the economy, your background, your upbringing, your lack of education or your past mistakes. For your life's plan is filled with promises that God wants to fulfill.

Let's look at a character in the bible named Moses as an example. Moses was chosen by God before He was born, to be the nation's deliverer. He did not apply for the job and yet his life's circumstances prepared him to BE and DO what God created Him to do. During the PROCESS, He would find out he was adopted. Wow, One day the son of a King and they next day the son of a slave. He was evicted from his home and went from the PALACE to the PITs! He was labeled a murderer; He was hated by those he thought were his countrymen and even more hated by his own people. He dealt with shame, disgrace, disbelief, dishonor, lack, hunger, abandonment, and driven to live in the wilderness as a vagabond with no kingdom and no home; and YET, none of those circumstances and situations changed who HE was and WHAT he was destined to do and become...He was a Deliverer!

But, while becoming who he was, Moses would often give God excuses for WHY he felt he was not ready to MAKE A DIFFERENCE... his background, his speech impediment, his past deeds, his outstanding warrant for arrest, lack of money or resources, no home, no supportive family or friends, no transportation and of course he didn't have a designer suite to wear to his presentation before the king! As a matter of fact, when he was told to step out, he did, without a plan. All he had was a command from God... to **"JUST DO IT"** (hmmm, sounds familiar... another billion-dollar idea!)

So, one day while giving God another excuse about WHY he couldn't do what God created him to do, God said, "MOSES... What do you have in your hand?" In the natural it appeared to be only a simple staff or a rod. God then said, throw what you have to the ground. When Moses did, it turned into a snake and Moses jumped away in fear. Now God said, grab the snake by the tail. In other words, **Moses that which you fear, grab by the tail, you take dominion over it. You subdue it and it will become the instrument that I will use to deliver My people.** Then God said and I continue paraphrasing, "Trust me Moses, if you use what you have in your hand... people will know, that the God of your ancestors appeared to you. They will know that I AM is with you and YOU will prosper in the thing I have sent you to do!"

Today I ask you, **What's in your hands?** What are your dreams, ideas, passions; your heart's desires. That song you wrote, but no one ever sang. The book waiting to be written, that the world needs to read; that witty invention; that recipe everyone brags on; that game; that gadget; that design; that business that can revolutionize this recession, that marketplace ministry that God will bring salvation to many who will never see the inside of a church until you introduce them to a Living Savior who wants them to use what's in their hands too! You need to know that, "God is able to do exceedingly, abundantly, above all we can ask or think, according to the power that is at WORK inside of you." The opportune word is At WORK, not sitting dormant or idle, procrastinating, embittered or upset, oppressed or depressed... but Doing what you were created to do. Something that others can use to better their way of life or to enjoy it. Then people will know that GOD appeared to you and is with you too! So again, I ask, **What's in your hands?**

Choosing to use what is in your hands does not come without a wilderness situation. And do not look for people to go in or up with you. It's nice when you have someone that can watch and wait, but know that if they don't, God is still asking what is in your hands. Not what is in theirs. No one will have the passion or resolve to do what God has created you to do. So, your success is not contingent upon people it has already been planned out by God. He said I know the plans I have for you, plans of good and not evil (plans of peace...) to bring you to an expected end. The question is are you in a posture or spirit of expectation? Do you Expect the Great?

You see In the wilderness is where the answers are birthed. Solutions are created. Problems are solved. Questions are answered. It was in the wilderness Moses went in as the son of a slave but came out KNOWING he was the leader and the deliverer of a nation. Who he was manifested into being once he encountered God? Where? In the wilderness. When God needs to rescue a nation, leaders are born, ideas are realized, a way is made out of no way!

In this time of a seemingly recession, there is something that ONLY you can do to recession proof your home, your neighborhood, your organization, your business, your city, your state, this nation... and become a deliverer for those you know and don't know! You are the answer we are waiting for! As a matter of fact, the earth is groaning for the sons of God to manifest and be all that we were created to BE! Now is the time to put to use.... **What's in YOUR Hands!**

Did you know that in times like these the world's greatest inventions were birthed? As a matter of fact, Inventions solves the need of necessities. During the Great Depression or in times of recession, people like you and I decided to give the world God's solution and revealed what was in their hands. In the greatest time of lack and poverty they took their ideas and made solutions to the world's economic crisis. And when the crisis was over, (because everything has a season and a time, and everything will change), they became very, very, very rich!!! Their legacy lives on today!

So, I ask you, what's in your hands today? God has given you a gift, a talent, an ability, a skill, a business... it will make room for you in whatever industry or arena you choose. What you must realize is, what you have in your hands was given to you by God. You did not even choose it, but God chose you for it. And He chose it not for you, but for others. Now the benefits you will receive will have great dividends and it is priceless!

Don't wait for the perfect conditions. Don't wait until you have enough money. Don't wait until your kids graduate from college or you go back to college. Don't wait until you get a better job or a promotion. Promotion comes not from the north or the east, but from the Lord. And in your due season and set time, when you humble yourself before God, He will promote you. Don't wait for a better car or home. Don't wait for permission, give yourself permission to be and do what you were created to do. Nothing beats a failure but a TRY!!! Don't be practical when it comes to your dreams; become radical. The Kingdom of God is suffering violence, but the violent (those who won't quit or give up) must take it by force!

Now I must caution you in advance, once you step out, like Moses, you will face others who will oppose you and not support you. They'll even try to talk you out of it! They'll put their rods on the ground just like you. But in the end, Moses' rod swallowed up the competition, WHY because there was no competition to begin with. What God has for you is for you! What God has ordained for you is for you. But FEAR (false evidence appearing real) won't let you do it. It will find a reason and a way to sabotage your success if you let it. So, I encourage you today to Have Faith in God! The God of all gods is with you. And if God be for you WHO can be against you! Sooner or later you will realize like Moses, the rod was never the instrument of power and ability... God was, and He still is... yesterday, today and forever!

Now at the set time, Moses did do what God created him to do. It did not come without hardship or pain, or even without trial and error, but it came just the same. In the end, with that same ROD in his hand, God used him and it, to part the Red Sea and deliver his people from the hands of a Pharaoh – (slavery, bondage, doubt, disbelief, fear, and failure) into a land of promise. He was the Deliverer!

Today is the day to take what's in your hands and use it for God's glory. You've been called to part whatever red sea that is blocking you and those you know from crossing over to your land of promise (prosperity, joy and freedom). You can make a difference. YES, YOU CAN! Because you have been empowered to know, that with God all things are possible to those that believe. Step out in faith......come on, release what's in your hands to the world! Meditate on God's Words to you... day & night. Write out the plan and then **step out in faith** knowing that He who has begun a good work will complete it. *"Faith is the substance of things hoped for. The evidence of things not seen!"* (Hebrew 11:1)

Just Do it!

Yesterday you dared to struggle...today dare to WIN!! Winners Make the Difference! Look at you.... You have that winning image!

My Success Is Not Negotiable. What about yours?

Let Us Pray:

Father I thank You for the seemingly impossibilities becoming possible. By faith all things are possible in You. Therefore, I take what is in my hands. These gifts, skills, talents that You have given to me and I rededicate them to You so that You can be glorified in the earth. I dismiss and disband from my heart and soul every thought, image and picture I have of unbelief, doubt and failure. There is no failure in heaven, therefore there is no failure in me. Every thought that has blocked or hindered me from going forward and doing or being what You have called me to do, I reject every spirit of doubt, fear and discouragement now in the name of Jesus Christ. I cancel every form of delay and I shall no longer be denied. You O' Lord will hasten to perform Your word concerning my life. I release the angels to harken to my words and roll away the stone of reproach and every hindrance to the manifestations of my breakthroughs now. I refuse to agree any longer that my situation of circumstance is impossible. No matter what it is, nothing is impossible for You. Lord demonstrate Your power. You are the God of impossibilities, grant me the desires of my heart this day, this month and this year. Cause me to revisit every word that I have spoken that contradicted and negates my progress. I renounce and denounce any words of agreement made with the enemy on any matter concerning my life. You have created me for a purpose. Lord let that purpose be fulfilled so You can be glorified in my life. The God of possibilities answer me today by fire. Burn everything that's not like You and let me come out as pure gold, ready to progress in success for the King and the Kingdom. Father, I thank You for my testimonies in advance.

And it is so. Manifest!

Soul Session Scripture: *"I can do all this through him who gives me strength."* Philippians 4:13

Soul Session Song: "Nothing is Impossible" by Planetshakers

SOUL SESSIONS - VOLUME 1: HEALING FOR THE SOUL

Daily Prayer Session

Father thank You for being Jehovah Rapha, our Healer, bringing forth divine healing for every person who reads *"Soul Sessions: Volume 1 – Healing For The Soul"* by Rhonda Ferguson-Lewis.

As I put on the full armor of God according to Ephesians 6:11, I take my stand against the devil's schemes and go forth in these prayers:

I thank You Lord, for opening my mind's eye, my subconscious thoughts and remembrance, to uncover Significant Emotional Events in my past, that have threatened to steal the joy of my present and future. I thank You for renewing my mind according to Romans 12:2. I declare the enemy's tactics are cut off now, in the name of Jesus!

In the mighty name of Jesus, I bind and rebuke each demonic spirit that was assigned to enforce spiritual attachments against me, and I command that each and every one of these demonic spirits be cast out and sent to dry places now, at this very moment. I cancel all demonic assignments made by the enemy against me and declare them null and void now!

God, I ask You in the name of Your precious Son Jesus to help my unbelief! Please forgive us for any lingering doubts in our hearts and minds. Strengthen me in Your word and to walk by faith and not by sight whole heartedly.

In the name of Jesus, I declare and decree that according to Psalm 103:1 I will bless the Lord with everything that is in me! I will bless His Holy name. No matter what comes my way, I will command my soul to have a "not my will, but yours" in my belly, and a "nevertheless" always on my tongue.

Father, please forgive me for any dishonest way in me. I recognize that dishonesty keeps me from receiving Your love and forgiveness. Lead me on Your everlasting path according to Psalm 139! Help me to reject dishonest, shameful deeds and underhanded methods. I declare I will establish truth on my lips and let it endure forever!

I declare and decree that, like Paul, in ALL things, I will THINK MYSELF HAPPY. I understand that You, my God, are concerned with everything that concerns me. For the JOY of the Lord is my strength!

Father, please search me and know my heart. I commit to loving You and loving others fiercely and genuinely. Remove the spaces between myself and others who I have harbored unforgiveness towards. I release the offense and I pray You forgive them. In the name of Jesus, I ask that You forgive me too as I purpose to walk in love, to seek peace, to live in agreement, and to conduct myself toward others in a manner that is pleasing to You.

Lord, I ask You to please forgive me for indecisions and even poor decisions I have made up until now. I no longer want to leave You out of any decision in my life. I thank You for filling me with Your Holy Spirit to lead and guide me. I declare that prayer will precede my decisions, that I will be anxious for nothing, and that I will take Your yoke upon me. I will seek Your kingdom first according to Matthew 6:33. I choose You above all today and always.

My God in Heaven, I have allowed my perceptions and what others think of me to rule and reign over my identity for too long. I ask Your forgiveness for seeking the approval of man before accepting my identity in YOU. I declare I will no longer value myself based on the opinions of this world, I will no longer practice self-rejection, and instead I will embrace your unconditional love. I will see You as You see me. I declare that I reject rejection because I can do all things through Christ who gives me strength according to Philippians 4:13.

I believe all things are possible with You Lord. I take my shield of faith and extinguish the flaming arrows of the evil one, in Jesus' name. I will trust in the plans You have for me, knowing they are good and have a purpose, according to Jeremiah 29:11. I declare You will not meet my expectations because you will EXCEED them!

I believe, and therefore I speak, and it is so. Manifest! In Jesus name, Amen!

Prayer Created By: Stephanie Pop, Member of Pearls of Wisdom 2019
Inspired by Chapters of Book: Soul Sessions: Volume 1 - Healing for the Soul

Soul Sessions: Volume 2 – Sexual Healing

Coming June 2020

To Book a Personal or Group

SOUL SESSION, Call 1-844-TWIMAGE or

Email: rfl@thewinningimage.net

Made in the USA
Columbia, SC
25 June 2019